CW01663119

STOICISM FOR THE 21ST CENTURY

AN EASY, PRACTICAL GUIDE TO OVERCOME CHALLENGES, IMPROVE DECISION MAKING, BUILD RESILIENCE, STRENGTHEN RELATIONSHIPS, AND FIND CALM IN A CHAOTIC WORLD

CHARLIE STEELE

Copyright © Charlie Steele - All rights reserved.

The content contained within this book may not be reproduced, duplicated or transmitted without direct written permission from the author or the publisher.

Under no circumstances will any blame or legal responsibility be held against the publisher, or author, for any damages, reparation, or monetary loss due to the information contained within this book. Either directly or indirectly. You are responsible for your own choices, actions, and results.

Legal Notice:

This book is copyright protected. This book is only for personal use. You cannot amend, distribute, sell, use, quote or paraphrase any part, or the content within this book, without the consent of the author or publisher.

Disclaimer Notice:

Please note the information contained within this document is for educational and entertainment purposes only. All effort has been executed to present accurate, up to date, and reliable, complete information. No warranties of any kind are declared or implied. Readers acknowledge that the author is not engaging in the rendering of legal, financial, medical or professional advice. The content within this book has been derived from various sources. Please consult a licensed professional before attempting any techniques outlined in this book.

By reading this document, the reader agrees that under no circumstances is the author responsible for any losses, direct or indirect, which are incurred as a result of the use of the information contained within this document, including, but not limited to, — errors, omissions, or inaccuracies.

CONTENTS

INTRODUCTION

In the chaos of a bustling airport, a young professional is caught in a whirlwind of emotions. With a delayed flight, a buzzing phone, and urgent emails pending, the weight of responsibilities seems to crush their spirits. As they slump into a chair, their eyes fall upon a small book in the airport bookstore: Marcus Aurelius's Meditations. Little do they know that this ancient text holds the key to navigating the complexities of modern life.

Like this professional, many of us find ourselves grappling with the challenges of the 21st century. We're bombarded with information, pressured to make swift decisions, and expected to maintain a delicate balance between our personal and professional lives. It's no wonder that stress, anxiety, and disconnection have become all too common. But what if I told you that the wisdom to overcome these obstacles lies in a philosophy that has endured for centuries? Many of the answers lay in the simplicity of approach and are within everyone's grasp. Even if strategies or approaches haven't worked for you before, embracing Stoicism for the 21st Century will allow you to apply timeless wisdom to today's challenges in order to thrive.

This book invites you to explore the teachings of Stoicism and discover how they can transform your life. Stoicism, a school of thought originating in Ancient Greece and Rome, offers a pragmatic approach to building mental resilience, improving relationships, making sound decisions, and finding tranquility amidst chaos. Despite the common misconception, Stoicism is not about being emotionless or indifferent but about developing the strength to face adversity with grace and wisdom.

Throughout these pages, we'll explore Stoicism's core principles and how they apply to today's challenges. From managing stress at work to cultivating meaningful relationships, from making tough choices to finding purpose in our daily routines, Stoicism provides a roadmap for navigating life's complexities. We'll examine the lives and teachings of renowned Stoic philosophers like Seneca, Epictetus, and Marcus Aurelius, gleaning insights that remain as relevant today as they were two millennia ago.

The practices and teachings are not earth-shattering revelations but practices and thought patterns that should feel wise, practical, and intuitive. You may recognize some of these approaches adopted by other schools of thought and modern psychology, but their origins lie in Stoic thinking. You may have learned about a range of approaches before but remained unsure about how they relate to your life, connect to each other, and extend beyond the theory. Therefore, this book is designed as more than just a philosophical exploration; it's a practical guide to integrating Stoicism into your daily life. Each chapter contains exercises, reflections, and real-world examples to help you implement Stoic principles. It also provides a more explicit framework for how these practices are connected and how they target different parts of your life. You'll learn to cultivate self-discipline, develop emotional resilience, improve decision-making, and build relationships. By the time you turn the final page, you'll have a toolkit of Stoic practices that you can apply to any situation.

The book can be used as you desire: it can be read in order from the first chapter. However, if you want clarity or support on certain areas of your life, navigate to these chapters using the contents guide to locate your preferred starting point. This guide is designed to be interactive and practical, allowing you to revisit key ideas or activities at relevant points in your life. If you reach a strategy or reflection exercise that you are not ready for, move on and return to it. However, by adopting a range of the proposed strategies, you will soon begin changing your thought patterns automatically and develop a connected and effective set of daily habits, thought patterns, and practices to enable you to thrive.

As Epictetus once said, "It's not what happens to you, but how you react to it that matters." This book is your companion on the journey to mastering your reactions and living a life of purpose and resilience. Whether you're a curious beginner or a seasoned seeker of wisdom, there's something here for you.

I have witnessed firsthand the transformative power of Stoicism, both in my own life and in the lives of countless others who I have supported. Yet, I remember the initial struggle to see its direct relevance to modern life. This book is the one I never had—the guide that would have made the journey clearer and more accessible. It bridges the gap between ancient wisdom and today's challenges, linking timeless Stoic principles to modern practices.

My passion lies in sharing this wisdom and helping you navigate life's challenges with greater ease and purpose. I have poured my heart and soul into creating a book that is both accessible and profound, designed to resonate with readers from all walks of life.

So, my friend, are you ready to embark on this journey of self-discovery and transformation? Are you prepared to embrace the wisdom of the ages and apply it to today's challenges? Are you ready to try some of the reflections and activities to improve your life? If so, let us begin. Together, we'll explore the depths of

Stoicism and unlock the secrets to a life well-lived. Your journey starts now.

1

UNDERSTANDING THE FOUNDATIONS OF STOICISM

"If a thing is in your own power, why do you do it? If it is in another's power, whom do you blame? The atoms or the gods? Either is foolish. Blame no one."

— EPICTETUS

One evening, in the heart of Athens, a young merchant named Zeno of Citium found himself stranded after a shipwreck. With no possessions to his name, he wandered into a local bookstore, where he stumbled upon a collection of Socratic dialogues. This encounter ignited a spark within Zeno, propelling him on a path that would lead to the creation of one of the most enduring philosophies in history: Stoicism. As you read this, you might wonder how the musings of ancient philosophers could relate to the complexities of modern life. Yet, this timeless wisdom offers us a lens through which to view our challenges with clarity and resilience.

1.1 THE ORIGINS OF STOICISM: FROM ANCIENT GREECE TO MODERN TIMES

Stoicism began in the bustling marketplaces of Athens around the 3rd century BCE. Zeno, having been inspired by the teachings of Socrates, established his school of thought at the Stoa Poikile, or the Painted Porch. This iconic location gave the philosophy its name. Zeno's teachings emphasized the importance of living in harmony with nature and reason, encouraging followers to pursue virtue over pleasure. His vision was to cultivate an inner strength capable of withstanding the unpredictability of life, fostering a community that prioritized rational thought and emotional equilibrium over impulsive behavior. Zeno's early disciples, such as Cleanthes and Chrysippus, carried forward his teachings, expanding Stoicism's reach and depth. They laid the philosophical groundwork that would later influence the Roman world, transforming Stoicism from a local Athenian curiosity into a guiding philosophy for emperors and citizens alike.

As the Roman Empire flourished, Stoicism found fertile ground in its culture, becoming central to the intellectual life of the era. Seneca, a statesman and philosopher, integrated Stoic principles into the fabric of Roman society. His writings, rich with insights on ethics and personal conduct, were designed to help individuals navigate the tumultuous waters of political and personal life. Therefore, although many influential statesmen adopted Stoicism, the teachings were just as relevant for everyday people. Thus, Seneca's eloquence and practicality made Stoicism accessible to both ordinary citizens and those in power.

Meanwhile, Marcus Aurelius, the philosopher king, penned his Meditations as a guide to living virtuously amidst the pressures of leadership. His reflections are a testament to the applicability of Stoicism in governance, offering timeless advice on maintaining moral integrity in the face of adversity. Then there was Epictetus, a formerly enslaved person whose teachings resonated with those seeking freedom from the tyranny of external circumstances. His emphasis on inner freedom and self-mastery has inspired countless seekers of wisdom, both then and now.

However, with the rise of Christianity and the shifting tides of power, Stoicism began to wane during the Middle Ages. Its influence faded as new theological paradigms emerged, reshaping the intellectual landscape of Europe. Yet, like a river that finds a new course, Stoicism resurfaced in the modern era, invigorated by its alignment with contemporary therapeutic practices and psychology. Cognitive-behavioral therapy (CBT), a popular form of psychotherapy today, draws heavily on Stoic principles, emphasizing the importance of perception in shaping emotional responses. Emotion regulation practices link back to this, too, as do many mindfulness and reflection practices. This philosophical resurgence has sparked renewed interest in Stoicism as a tool for emotional regulation and personal development, integrating it into modern self-help literature and mindfulness practices.

This journey from Ancient Greece to modern therapy underscores the timeless nature of Stoicism. Its teachings on resilience, rationality, and emotional regulation are not relics of the past but valuable resources for addressing today's challenges. Stoicism offers a steady compass, whether it's the stress of a demanding job, the complexities of interpersonal relationships, or the existential questions of life's purpose. It guides you toward a life of virtue, helping you navigate the tumultuous seas of modern existence with grace and wisdom. In the following chapters, we'll explore how to integrate these ancient teachings into your daily life, providing practical exercises and insights to enhance your well-being and decision-making.

In the remainder of this chapter, we will explore some of Stoicism's defining principles. These principles may appear again in later chapters, where their influence is critical for understanding specific strategies or approaches.

1.2 THE DICHOTOMY OF CONTROL: MASTERING WHAT YOU CAN CHANGE

Imagine a day that starts with a perfectly planned schedule, but as it unfolds, unexpected events throw everything into disarray. The project deadline gets moved up, a family emergency arises, and the weather turns sour just before an important meeting. It's enough to make anyone feel overwhelmed. Yet, Stoicism offers a guiding principle that can bring clarity amidst chaos: the dichotomy of control. This concept divides life into two simple categories: what we can control and what we cannot. By focusing only on the factors within our control, we conserve energy, reduce stress, and achieve a sense of calm even when the world seems unpredictable.

The wisdom of the dichotomy of control is profound in its simplicity. Consider what lies within your control: your thoughts, actions, and reactions to your emotions. These are the areas where your influence is most potent and where your efforts should be concentrated. The weather, the economy, and other people's actions are all beyond your control and, as such, do not warrant your concern. This Stoic principle encourages you to focus on shaping your responses rather than fretting over external events. By doing so, you cultivate a mindset prioritizing rational action over fruitless worry, freeing your mind from the shackles of what-ifs and maybes.

Although seemingly simple, the Stoic principle of focusing only on what is within our control is one of the most effective tools for reducing stress and maintaining overall well-being. Research suggests that a significant portion of our daily energy—over 70%—is expended on concerns beyond our control, leading to unnecessary stress and mental fatigue. When we fixate on uncontrollable factors, such as external events or other people's actions, we trigger a physiological stress response. This response, initiated in the hypothalamic-pituitary-adrenal (HPA) axis, releases cortisol and other stress hormones, which, over time, can contribute to chronic inflammation, cardiovascular issues, and mental health struggles.

Even minor frustrations, such as getting stuck in traffic, can elicit this response. While the event itself is neutral, our emotional reaction—frustration, anger, or impatience—activates the body's stress system, draining cognitive and emotional resources. If this pattern continues unchecked, it can lead to prolonged low-grade stress, a known contributor to anxiety, depression, and even weakened immune function. This, unfortunately, is the state that many of us exist in without realizing it. By practicing cognitive reframing, as Stoicism encourages, we can shift our attention away from what we cannot change, conserving mental energy and fostering resilience in the face of daily stressors.

The practical applications of this principle are countless. In the workplace, for example, you may be burdened by the stress of a demanding job where deadlines shift and clients have unpredictable needs. By applying the dichotomy of control, you can focus on your work ethic, what actions you take, and how you communicate with colleagues rather than the ever-changing demands. This shift in focus can alleviate anxiety, allowing you to approach each task with clarity and purpose. Similarly, when life throws unexpected challenges, such as a sudden illness or financial setback, prioritizing your reactions and stepping forward will empower you to face adversity with resilience. You won't waste energy fighting against uncontrollable circumstances; instead, you can adapt and respond with thoughtful actions.

How do you do this? The approach is deceptively simple yet profoundly powerful if adopted correctly. Initially, it begins with you noticing that an event has caused a significant emotion within you. Next, question yourself: Is it something that I can control? If it isn't, accept the event, say it aloud, and even acknowledge it as a fact, but remind yourself that you won't let it have power over you or your body. If needed, distract yourself at this point to help you to focus on an alternative. Follow the steps in the exercise below to support you with this.

Understanding the dichotomy of control and adopting this mindset offers significant psychological benefits. It reduces anxiety by disentangling your emotional well-being from things you cannot change. This newfound tranquility fosters enhanced decision-making as you become more adept at assessing situations objectively and acting on what truly matters. Imagine a professional thriving in a high-pressure environment, maintaining composure while others falter. By embracing the dichotomy of control, this individual can channel their efforts into delivering quality work and fostering positive relationships whilst unaffected by external noise. Their success stems from the ability to focus solely on what they can influence, illustrating the power of this Stoic tenet.

Consider Walt Disney, who faced significant setbacks early in his career. These included losing creative control of Oswald the Rabbit and having MGM reject Mickey Mouse, fearing audiences wouldn't accept a cartoon mouse. Rather than dwelling on these losses, Disney focused on what he could control: improving his animation and storytelling. His perseverance and disciplined mindset ultimately led to Mickey Mouse becoming one of the world's most recognizable characters.

Disney's journey exemplifies Stoic resilience—choosing response over reaction, maintaining emotional discipline, and transforming adversity into an opportunity for growth. His success underscores the power of focusing on controllable factors, proving that obstacles can become stepping stones rather than roadblocks.

Reflection Activity: Embracing Control

Take a moment to reflect on a recent situation that caused you stress or strong emotions. On one side of the page, write down the elements within your control, and on the other side, those beyond your control. Try to make this list as comprehensive as possible.

Once you've identified what you can control, focus on these aspects. These are the areas where your energy should be directed. On the other hand, the elements beyond your control should be acknowledged but not given your energy. Dwelling on uncontrollable elements only fuels unnecessary worry and drains your mental resources.

What should you do if thoughts about uncontrollable aspects arise?

The key is reframing your thoughts in the moment.

Step 1: Identify whether the situation or element is within your control or not.

Step 2: For controllable aspects, take deliberate action to resolve or improve the situation. For uncontrollable aspects, acknowledge the thought and remind yourself that you cannot change it. Once acknowledged, consciously decide to release that thought and stop investing mental energy in it.

Step 3: Use this exercise to reframe future challenges, applying the dichotomy of control as a tool to guide your actions. Over time, this will become more automatic, reducing the need for structured reflection.

This isn't an overnight change; it requires deliberate practice. However, with time, it will become a natural response. By consistently applying this principle, you'll find greater peace and efficiency in how you approach daily challenges.

1.3 VIRTUE ETHICS: LIVING ACCORDING TO NATURE AND REASON

Within the heart of Stoicism lies the profound belief in aligning one's life with nature and reason, a path illuminated by the pursuit of virtue. To the Stoics, living virtuously was not a lofty ideal reserved for philosophers but a practical approach to life accessible to all. This philosophy is anchored by the four cardinal virtues: wisdom, courage, justice, and temperance. Each serves as a pillar supporting the structure of a well-lived life. Wisdom, the first of these virtues, involves discerning the true nature of things, making informed decisions, and understanding the consequences of one's actions. It encourages a thoughtful engagement with the world, urging us to seek knowledge and apply it judiciously. On the other hand, courage is the strength to face fears and adversities and the ability to act rightly in the face of societal pressures or personal doubts. *It is not the absence of fear but the realization that some things are more important than fear itself.*

Justice, as conceptualized by the Stoics, extends beyond legal systems and into the realm of moral fairness and integrity. It calls for actions that honor the common good, fostering a sense of community and empathy. Lastly, temperance teaches moderation, encouraging self-control and balance in desires and actions. This virtue helps us navigate the temptations of excess, guiding us toward a life governed by restraint and thoughtful choices. These virtues form a compass, orienting us toward a harmonious existence with the natural world and our rational nature.

These virtues manifest in various scenarios in today's fast-paced environment, offering guidance amidst chaos. Wisdom might appear in the form of a manager who, when faced with a difficult decision, chooses not to rush but to gather all relevant information, weighing the potential outcomes carefully. Courage is seen in the individual who stands up against unethical workplace practices despite potential backlash. Justice can be witnessed in promoting equality, ensuring that decisions and policies reflect fairness. Temperance emerges in prioritizing health, avoiding overindulgence, and maintaining a balanced lifestyle even when faced with excess. These virtues are not abstract concepts but practical tools that can be cultivated and applied to everyday life.

To nurture these virtues, consider engaging in exercises that foster self-reflection and growth. Examine instances of justice in your interactions with others. Reflect on your ability to exercise temperance, identifying areas where moderation was needed. Role-playing scenarios can also be beneficial, allowing you to practice virtuous responses in a controlled environment and preparing you for real-life challenges. These practices encourage you to internalize the virtues central to Stoicism.

History provides us with vivid examples of these virtues in action. The Roman Emperor, Marcus Aurelius, embodied justice in his leadership, often prioritizing the welfare of his people over personal gain. His commitment to fairness and responsibility is a timeless example of Stoic virtue in governance. Seneca, another prominent Stoic philosopher, wrote extensively about courage, particularly in adversity. His life, marked by political intrigue and personal trials, demonstrated resilience and determination. His writings inspire those seeking to cultivate inner strength and face life's challenges with fortitude.

Each figure provides a window into the living application of Stoic virtues, illustrating how these timeless principles can guide us through the complexities of modern life. By embracing these virtues, we align ourselves with the natural order, tapping into a wellspring of resilience and wisdom that can transform our existence.

Reflection Activity: Your Stoic Compass

Reflect on how the four Stoic virtues—wisdom, courage, justice, and temperance—are present in your life:

- **Wisdom:** Where do you make informed decisions? Where could you seek more knowledge?
- **Courage:** When have you faced fears or challenges? Where could you act with more bravery?

- **Justice:** How do you practice fairness? Are there situations where you could stand up for what is right?
- **Temperance:** Where do you show moderation? Are there areas where you need more balance or self-control?

Set small, actionable goals to strengthen each virtue in your daily life, ensuring they guide your decisions and actions.

1.4 THE ROLE OF LOGOS: UNDERSTANDING THE RATIONAL ORDER

In the vast expanse of the universe, Stoics found a guiding principle known as logos. This concept, rooted deeply in Stoic philosophy, represents the rational structure that underpins all existence. Imagine logos as an intricate tapestry woven with threads of reason and order, providing coherence to life's seemingly random events. For the Stoics, logos was not just an abstract idea; it was the essence of rationality, the divine logic that orchestrates the cosmos. By understanding and aligning with this rational order, individuals could find their place within the universe, embracing a harmonious existence.

This is a fundamental principle for those feeling a lack of purpose or a disconnect from the world. As the Stoics envisioned, participating in the rational cosmos meant living by this universal reason. It was about acknowledging that our lives are part of a larger, interconnected whole, a cosmic community governed by laws far more significant than our desires. This perspective encourages us to perceive our actions not in isolation but as ripples in the vast ocean of life. Each choice we make, every action we take, has a resonance that echoes through the universe, contributing to the symphony of existence. By aligning our actions with logos, we find personal peace and contribute to universal harmony.

Understanding logos offers a profound sense of interconnectedness. It invites us to see our place in the world as part of an intricate dance of cause and effect, where our actions are both influenced by and influential to the greater whole. This alignment fosters a sense of tranquility as we learn to flow with the natural order rather than resist it. It teaches us to seek wisdom and insight, act with intention and purpose, and always be mindful of our decisions' impact on ourselves and the world around us. This alignment with logos becomes a compass, guiding us through the complexities of life with a steady hand.

Incorporating logos into daily life involves practical steps that attune us to its logical flow. Mindfulness practices become a powerful tool in this journey, allowing us to quiet the noise of the external world and tune into the rhythm of reason. We can cultivate a growth mindset that embraces logic and inquiry through meditation and reflective practices. This mindset encourages us to question assumptions, seek understanding, and approach challenges with a calm, rational perspective. Doing so creates a fertile ground for personal growth, where reason and intuition coexist in a balanced dance.

The influence of logos extends beyond philosophy and into the realms of science and rational inquiry. Stoicism's emphasis on reason laid the groundwork for scientific exploration, encouraging a systematic pursuit of knowledge and truth. Modern interpretations of logos continue to inform philosophical thought, bridging the gap between ancient wisdom and contemporary understanding. In a world often guided by emotion and impulse, logos stands as a beacon of clarity, urging us to embrace the rational order that connects us all.

To illustrate the power of logos, consider the serenity found in nature's cycles. The changing seasons, the ebb and flow of tides, and the daily rise and set of the sun follow a rhythm dictated by the universe's rational structure. By observing these patterns, we learn to appreciate the beauty of order and predictability, finding peace in knowing we are part of something greater. This same peace is available to us when we align our lives with logos, embracing the wisdom of the Stoics as a guiding light in our pursuit of a life well-lived.

Reflection Activity: Logos and the Kindness Ripple Effect

Logos, or rationality, is reflected in the ripple effect of small acts of kindness. Even the simplest gestures can create waves of positivity that extend far beyond the initial action.

Activity: Kindness Ripple Effect In Action

Commit to **one small act of kindness each day for a week**—a smile, holding the door, helping someone, or paying for a stranger's coffee.

Reflect on the Impact:

- How did your actions affect others?
- Did you notice a shift in their mood or in the environment around you?
- How did practicing kindness help you feel more connected to the greater whole?

By consistently engaging in kindness, you'll see how small choices contribute to a larger sense of goodwill and community, reinforcing the Stoic principle that we are all part of something greater.

1.5 MEMENTO MORI: EMBRACING MORTALITY TO LIVE FULLY

Have you ever read or heard about the regrets of the dying or reflections of those on their deathbeds? Although it may sound frightening, many realize that they only start living and appreciating how life is finite when they are close to death. What if we could acknowledge this much earlier in our lives in order to understand the impermanence of our existence and appreciate life fully? In the quiet of the night, as the world settles into a hush, a profound practice beckons us to reflect on the inevitable truth of our existence: Memento Mori, the reminder of our mortality. This Stoic practice invites us to contemplate the impermanent nature of life, not as a morbid exercise but as a powerful tool for appreciating the moments we have. By acknowledging that life is finite, we are urged to focus on what truly matters. This contemplation strips away the trivialities and distractions, revealing the core of living fully and authentically.

For the Stoics, death was not a distant specter to be feared but a natural part of the human experience. They taught that embracing our mortality liberates us from the shackles of fear, allowing us to engage with life more deeply and purposefully. This perspective shifts our focus from what we might lose to what we have right now, encouraging us to invest our time and energy wisely. By living with the awareness that each day could be our last, we are inspired to prioritize our values, nurture meaningful relationships, and pursue our passions with vigor and intention.

Embracing mortality doesn't mean living in constant dread; instead, it is about reducing the fear of death through acceptance. Question yourself: What would you do today if you knew your time was limited? When we accept the inevitability of our end, we can confront it with courage and tranquility. This acceptance fosters a profound sense of peace, freeing us from the anxiety that often accompanies the unknown. We learn to let go of the futile pursuit of permanence and savor life's transient beauty. By doing so, we cultivate a life rich in purpose and fulfillment, grounded in the present moment.

To integrate Memento Mori into daily life, consider adopting reflective practices that bring this concept into focus. Begin each day with a moment of gratitude, acknowledging the gift of life and the opportunities it presents. Engage in visualization exercises where you imagine how you might feel if today were your last. What would you want to accomplish? Who would you like to spend time with? These reflections help clarify your priorities, guiding your actions toward what truly matters. Such practices enhance your appreciation for life and strengthen your resolve to live according to your values.

Historical figures offer us a window into the power of Memento Mori. In his Meditations, Marcus Aurelius often reflected on death as a way to guide his thoughts and actions toward virtue. He recognized the fleeting nature of life and used this awareness to cultivate a life of meaning and integrity. In modern times, many individuals have found purpose through contemplating their mortality, using this insight to drive personal growth and transformation. By facing the reality of death, they have discovered a renewed zest for life, embracing each moment with gratitude and grace.`

Reflection Activity: Gratitude in Practice

Gratitude is a powerful practice that has been scientifically proven to enhance well-being, resilience, and happiness. Research indicates that individuals who consciously count their blessings tend to be happier and less depressed. It is the act of acknowledging what we are thankful for in the present moment, helping us fully appreciate the richness of life. Additionally, studies have shown that practicing gratitude can lead to improved health, including better heart health, lower blood pressure, and reduced systemic inflammation.

Begin to explore this by keeping a gratitude journal by your bedside. Each day, write down three things you're thankful for—big or small. Simple comforts, like a warm meal or clean water, are often overlooked.

Now, reflect: *If today were my last day, would I change anything? Would I take a risk or embrace an opportunity I've been avoiding?* Let gratitude inspire intentional action in your life.

As we conclude this reflection, let us carry the wisdom of Memento Mori with us. May it inspire us to live not in fear of what is to come but in celebrating what is. Let us honor the present, cherish our loved ones, and passionately pursue our dreams, knowing that life is a precious gift to savor. Ultimately, not the length of our days defines us but the depth of our experiences and the love we share.

We have explored some key underpinnings of Stoic thinking in Chapter 1. As we move to Chapter 2, to explore emotional resilience, use the quote below for a final reflection.

"He who fears death will never do anything worthy of a living man."

— SENECA, LETTERS TO LUCILIUS

2

EMOTIONAL RESILIENCE THROUGH STOIC PRACTICES

"Difficulties strengthen the mind, as labor does the body."

— SENECA, ON PROVIDENCE, 5.7-8

Have you ever felt overwhelmed by emotions like rage, anger, or sadness, as if they were taking over? These feelings are natural, but how we respond to them depends on our emotional intelligence. Like children, adults experience emotions, but the difference lies in how we manage them. When a boss yells, a stranger swears, or someone cuts you off in traffic, they're expressing emotions unfiltered—much like a child. What sets some adults apart is their ability to regulate emotions through emotional intelligence, a skill developed over time rather than being innate. Despite its impact on life satisfaction, relationships, success, and even wealth, emotional intelligence is rarely taught in schools and often learned through trial and error. The good news is that with practice, anyone can strengthen their emotional intelligence. This chapter explores how to cultivate it, build resilience, and embrace your fate.

2.1 EMOTIONAL INTELLIGENCE: CONQUERING THE GROWLING WOLF

A useful metaphor for understanding the connection between our thoughts and emotions is a growling wolf. When faced with an external stimulus, the wolf instinctively leaps into action, reacting almost immediately. However, the key word here is almost.

What many people realize only later, or sometimes never, is that there is a brief pause between the stimulus and our emotional reaction. This pause, though subtle, holds immense power. It is the space where emotion regulation begins, allowing us to choose our response rather than being ruled by impulse. Mastering this pause is fundamental to developing emotional intelligence and cultivating greater control over our reactions.

Imagine this: You're walking down the street when someone bumps into you—hard. You instinctively jump back, anger rising, and you start shouting, "Hey! What did you do that for, you idiot!" As you turn around, you see it's a small woman who accidentally tripped over a bump in the ground. She hadn't meant to hurt you, and in fact, she was injured herself. As you take in the situation, you feel a sense of shame, even though the anger is still bubbling up inside you.

This is where the pause comes in. The space between the stimulus (the bump), the emotion (anger), and your reaction is crucial. If you train yourself to pause long enough, you can begin to control your emotional responses. With practice, you'll stop reacting impulsively and instead respond in ways that align with your values and the person you want to be.

You may be wondering where this emotional reactivity comes from. Our brains are wired to respond quickly to stimuli, especially when they trigger emotions. This rapid response system evolved to help us survive. For instance, the amygdala, a key part of the brain, plays a vital role in processing emotional responses, such as fear or anger, when we perceive threats. The amygdala reacts quickly, often before we are consciously aware of the danger, helping us respond fast to potential harm. This is why, in moments of stress or confrontation, we tend to have quick, emotional reactions. However, in the modern world, many of these automatic responses are no longer necessary for survival. Fostering a pause between the stimulus and our reaction allows us to override this automatic emotional response. It is crucial to learn how to foster this pause as chronic emotional reactivity can lead to sustained cortisol release, increasing stress levels and negatively impacting both mental and physical health. By creating space, we give ourselves the time to engage the prefrontal cortex, which regulates and moderates the amygdala's impulses, allowing us to assess the situation thoughtfully and respond rationally.

This pause not only helps us manage emotional reactivity but also leads to more intentional and measured responses. Research has shown that practicing emotional regulation strategies can alter brain activity, specifically in the prefrontal cortex and amygdala, improving our ability to handle emotions effectively. By practicing this pause, we develop greater emotional intelligence, leading to more thoughtful, rational, and controlled reactions in challenging situations.

Again, this concept is powerful in its simplicity but takes time to develop to automaticity. To improve your ability with this, complete the reflection activity below on a recent experience where you felt emotionally triggered. Once you feel confident with the approach and what is involved, begin to try this out in daily situations. Remember that, initially, you might only catch the emotion after the stimulus-emotion-response process has already been completed. Over time, however, through regular practice, you will be able to build this into an automatic skill, allowing for time to evaluate your response before reacting.

Reflection Activity: Stimulus-Emotion-Response

Think of a recent moment when you reacted instinctively without pausing. This exercise helps you break down that reaction and cultivate awareness.

1. **Identify the Stimulus:** What triggered your emotional response? A comment? A situation?
2. **Examine Your Emotion:** What did you feel—anger, frustration, fear? How intense was it?
3. **Pause and Reflect:**
    - Was my reaction proportional?
    - Can I control this situation, or is it beyond my influence?
    - How can I respond in a way that aligns with my values?
4. **Evaluate Your Response:** Did your reaction reflect your best self, or was it automatic?

Practice: Try applying this approach to past situations first, then use it in real time. The more you pause and reflect, the more control you gain over your responses.

By practicing this process, you'll gradually build the skill to respond more thoughtfully, turning emotional reactions into deliberate, controlled responses that reflect your best self.

2.2 APATHEIA: MANAGING EMOTIONS WITHOUT SUPPRESSION

Imagine a serene lake, its surface unruffled by the winds that blow across it. This image captures the essence of apatheia, a Stoic ideal that speaks to being undisturbed by the turbulence of excessive emotions while remaining fully engaged with life. Apatheia is not about numbing oneself to feelings but distinguishing between productive emotional responses and those that cloud judgment. Unlike emotional suppression, which involves pushing emotions away, apatheia requires understanding and navigating them with rationality. By approaching emotions as signals to be interpreted rather than impulses to be acted upon, you embrace reason as a guide. This builds on our understanding of creating the pause between stimulus-emotion-response and extends our understanding of the emotional element, allowing emotions to inform without overpowering our decisions. Thus, rationality becomes the anchor, helping maintain a steady course through life's emotional seas.

Extensive research has examined emotions, revealing a crucial insight: emotions are signals, not mere impulses—contrary to common belief. Understanding this distinction is essential for emotional awareness and regulation.

When we experience anger, frustration, or sadness, these emotions serve as internal signals that something in our environment or within ourselves requires attention. Rather than prompting immediate action (unless in a life-or-death situation), emotions act as indicators, urging us to reflect and address underlying issues thoughtfully. Recognizing emotions as valuable feedback rather than automatic reactions empowers us to respond with intention rather than impulse.

Studies have consistently supported the power of cognitive reappraisal, where individuals reinterpret the meaning of stimuli to modify their emotional response, finding it leads to significant improvements in the subjective experience of emotions. Additionally, research indicates that reappraisal activates cognitive control regions and modulates the amygdala, suggesting that this strategy can help regulate emotional responses by engaging brain areas associated with rational decision-making and reducing the influence of regions linked to emotional reactivity. By consistently practicing this reframing technique, you can transform your emotional experiences into opportunities for personal growth and resilience, fostering a balanced and thoughtful approach to life's challenges.

Another effective strategy that supports the process of cognitive reframing is emotion labeling—acknowledging and naming the emotion you are experiencing, even aloud if necessary. However, rather than letting it take control, remind yourself that it is only a signal and ask yourself: *Will allowing this emotion to consume me be beneficial?* If the answer is no, practice detachment.

You can achieve this detachment by **physically** stepping away from the situation, changing your environment, or taking a walk. Alternatively, you can **mentally** detach by redirecting your thoughts to a positive memory, visualizing a place of calm and stability, or practicing relevant mindfulness approaches.

Balancing emotional detachment with engagement requires setting healthy boundaries. It's about knowing when to step back and when to lean in. Emotional boundaries protect your well-being, allowing you to remain open to others without becoming overwhelmed. Practicing empathy within these boundaries ensures you connect with others while retaining your composure. Empathy, in this context, involves understanding others' feelings without absorbing them as your own. It's about listening and responding with compassion while maintaining your emotional equilibrium. By practicing this balance, you engage meaningfully with the world, nurturing relationships without losing yourself.

Consider the ancient philosopher Epictetus, who taught extensively about maintaining peace in adversity. He believed that true freedom comes from within, unaffected by external circumstances. For Epictetus, apatheia was about recognizing what lies within your control and what does not. His teachings emphasized that while you cannot change the actions of others, you can choose your reactions.

This perspective empowers you to maintain inner peace, regardless of the chaos around you. In modern settings, professionals often find themselves in high-pressure environments where emotional regulation is crucial. Take, for example, a healthcare worker in a bustling emergency room. The ability to remain calm and focused amidst chaos enhances performance and ensures compassionate patient care. By practicing apatheia, these individuals manage their emotions effectively, delivering care with precision and empathy.

Reflection Activity: Managing Emotions with Cognitive Reframing

Emotions are signals, not obstacles. By reframing them, you turn them into tools for growth rather than sources of distress.

Steps to Reframe Emotions:

1. **Pause and Observe:** Acknowledge the emotion without judgment.
2. **Identify the Signal:** Ask yourself:
   - What is this emotion telling me?
   - What needs my attention or action?
3. **Reframe the Emotion:** See it as a guide. Anxiety may signal a need for growth; anger might highlight the need for boundaries.
4. **Choose Your Response:** Act in a way that aligns with your values and well-being.

To reinforce this, practice physical or mental detachment—step away, breathe, or shift perspective. The more you practice, the more control you gain over your emotions.

Here are two short activities to illustrate **physical** and **mental** detachment techniques:

Physical Detachment Activity: The Reset Walk

1. **Recognize the Emotion:** Pause and acknowledge what you're feeling.
2. **Label It:** Say aloud or mentally, *"I am feeling [emotion] right now."*
3. **Step Away:** If possible, change your environment—take a brief walk, even just around the room.
4. **Engage Your Senses:**
   - Notice five objects.
   - Listen for three distinct sounds.
   - Feel the ground beneath you or the air around you.
5. **Reassess:** After a few minutes, check if the intensity has decreased. Can you now respond with clarity?

Mental Detachment Activity: The Calm Visualization

1. **Pause & Breathe:** Close your eyes and take a slow, deep breath.
2. **Label the Emotion:** Say to yourself, *"I am feeling [emotion]."*
3. **Shift Focus:** Picture a calming place—a beach, forest, or a favorite peaceful spot.
4. **Engage Your Senses:**
   - Visualize the colors and shapes.
   - Imagine the sounds—waves, birds, soft music.
   - Feel the warmth of the sun or a gentle breeze.
5. **Detach:** With each breath, let the emotion fade like a wave retreating. After a minute or two, open your eyes and return to the present.

Both techniques help to quickly create space between emotion and response, giving you the clarity to choose how to proceed. They also offer you an alternative strategy to use if cognitive reframing has not allowed you to fully disengage from the overwhelming emotion.

2.3 CULTIVATING ATARAXIA: ACHIEVING INNER CALM

In the realm of Stoic philosophy, ataraxia represents a state of serene calmness, an oasis of peace amidst the turbulence of life. It is a mental stillness, free from the clamor of distress and worry. This calm is not apathy, which implies a lack of feeling or concern. Ataraxia, by contrast, involves an active engagement with life, but one that is unperturbed by the chaos around us. It is a state where you can maintain equilibrium regardless of external circumstances. The Stoics regarded ataraxia as a cornerstone of their teachings, a prerequisite for living a life aligned with nature and reason. Achieving this state allows you to experience life's ups and downs with equanimity, ensuring that neither elation nor despair can disrupt your inner peace.

Mindfulness and meditation are often essential for achieving this state and will be explored further in the activity below. However, when engaging with exercises in the pursuit of ataraxia, despite your best efforts, barriers to tranquility may arise. Intrusive thoughts, for instance, can disrupt your calm, swirling in your mind like a relentless storm. When these thoughts appear, recognize them for what they are—temporary disturbances. Instead of engaging, observe them with detachment, allowing them to pass like clouds across the sky. A method to do this is to say out loud "another thought" every time one arises. Identifying and recognizing that another thought has arisen strengthens your ability to remain mindful. Rather than finding these intrusive thoughts frustrating, you should congratulate yourself on being able to identify them without allowing them to take over your thoughts. The mere fact of noticing the thought is demonstrating your improving skill.

The benefits of achieving ataraxia ripple through all aspects of your life. Being able to achieve ataraxia allows you to navigate critical situations across all aspects of your life with enhanced focus and clarity. Decisions become less about reacting to immediate pressures and more about thoughtful consideration. This clarity extends to relationships, where calm and composed interactions lead to deeper connections and understanding. You can listen more intently, respond with empathy, and resolve conflicts with grace. Ataraxia transforms how you perceive challenges and engage with the world, fostering an environment of mutual respect and harmony.

Practical Activities:

Achieving Calm Through Breathwork

Breathwork helps reduce stress, improve mood, and support overall well-being by activating the body's relaxation response.

Benefits of Breathwork:

- Lowers stress and anxiety by reducing heart rate and blood pressure.
- Enhances emotional regulation and resilience.
- Improves sleep by promoting relaxation.

Breathwork Exercises to Try:

- **Box Breathing:** Inhale for 4 seconds, hold for 4, exhale for 4, hold for 4. Repeat. *Boosts focus and relaxation.*
- **Diaphragmatic Breathing:** Inhale deeply, letting your belly rise; exhale slowly. *Encourages full oxygen exchange and reduces tension.*
- **4-7-8 Breathing:** Inhale for 4 seconds, hold for 7, exhale for 8. Repeat. *Acts as a natural calming technique.*

Tip: Practice daily or use breathwork for quick relief when feeling overwhelmed.

Achieving Calm Through Mindfulness

Mindfulness, rooted in Stoic teachings, helps you stay present and cultivate inner peace. Here are two simple exercises:

1. Mindfulness Body Scan (10-15 min)

- Settle in: Sit or lie down, breathe deeply, and relax.
- Scan your body: Bring awareness from head to toe, noticing sensations without judgment.
- Embrace stillness: Observe your breath, releasing any tension.

2. Mindfulness Walk

- Pause before walking: Take deep breaths and notice your posture.
- Engage your senses: Observe colors, sounds, scents, and textures.
- Walk with awareness: Focus on each step and your breath, releasing distractions.
- Close with gratitude: Pause to appreciate something around you.

These simple practices can help ground you in the present, fostering clarity and calm in your daily life.

2.4 CULTIVATING EMOTIONAL RESILIENCE THROUGH NEGATIVE VISUALIZATION

As we develop our skills in emotional regulation and cultivating inner calm, it is essential to remember that anxieties and worries can sometimes surface and that this is part of being human. At the source of some of this anxiety is a worry of the unknown, but Stoics have developed a practice to mitigate this in order to feel prepared and thus more emotionally resilient.

Picture yourself standing at the edge of a calm sea, the horizon stretching endlessly before you. The waves gently lap at your feet, each one a reminder of the vastness and unpredictability of life. In this moment of reflection, you consider the challenges you might face tomorrow, next week, or even years from now. This contemplation is not a source of anxiety but a deliberate practice known as negative visualization. Rooted in the teachings of Stoicism, negative visualization invites you to imagine potential adversities, allowing you to mentally prepare for them and, paradoxically, deepen your appreciation for the present.

Negative visualization is not about dwelling on catastrophe but adopting a proactive mindset. It involves envisioning the worst-case scenarios that life might throw your way. By confronting these possibilities head-on, you reduce the fear that often accompanies the unknown. As you visualize these scenarios, you understand that adversity is a natural aspect of life, an inevitable part of the human experience that cannot be avoided, only managed. This practice helps build a robust mental framework, enabling you to face challenges calmly and rationally. It also allows you to think of practical solutions to adverse outcomes in order to feel more prepared. Whilst completing this activity, it is also essential to build on your understanding of the dichotomy of control. This was a concept that we explored in Chapter 1 (1.2). When contemplating future scenarios, it is crucial to keep these in perspective in terms of what you can and cannot control. By keeping this reflection as a key component of your visualization, you are bringing rationality to the reflection, too.

Research supports the psychological benefits of negative visualization, a technique rooted in Stoic philosophy. By contemplating potential adversities, individuals can enhance mental resilience and foster gratitude for their current circumstances. This practice shifts focus from fearing possible adverse events to appreciating present positives, thereby improving overall well-being. A study published in the *Journal of Positive Psychology* examined the effects of mentally subtracting positive events—imagining the absence of significant life occurrences —on gratitude and happiness. The findings revealed that participants who engaged in this form of negative visualization experienced heightened gratitude and a greater appreciation for their current lives. Modern psychology fully acknowledges the role of such techniques in building psychological resilience. By envisioning potential challenges, you can prepare yourself emotionally and mentally, leading to increased resilience when facing actual difficulties. When adversity does strike, you're not caught off guard. Instead, you're equipped with the resilience to navigate these trials with composure and clarity.

To incorporate negative visualization into your daily routine, consider a point in your day, such as the start of your day, for a brief meditation on potential challenges. As you sip your morning coffee, spend a few minutes picturing the obstacles you might encounter. This could be a difficult conversation at work or an unforeseen personal issue. By visualizing these events, you prepare your mind to handle them with grace and poise. In the evening, end your day with a reflection on the challenges you avoided or overcame, allowing gratitude to fill the space where anxiety might have lingered. If significant issues or worries arise, remember to use the reflection activity from Chapter 1 (1.2) to identify controllable and uncontrollable factors. This will help you frame your thinking so that you are ready for the day in terms of where you will focus your energies and allow you to release elements out of your control. This practice grounds you in the present and strengthens your emotional resilience over time.

Throughout history, individuals have successfully employed negative visualization to navigate their lives. In his letters, the philosopher Seneca often discussed the power of foresight. He believed that by contemplating potential misfortunes, one could mitigate fear and live a more fulfilling life. Seneca's writings offer valuable insights into the practical application of this Stoic technique. Modern leaders across various fields use visualization to prepare for crises. They imagine possible setbacks and develop strategies to address them, ensuring they remain composed under pressure and can lead effectively.

Reflection Activity: Negative Visualization

To begin your practice of negative visualization, set aside five minutes each morning or at an appropriate point in the day. Find a quiet space and close your eyes. Picture the day ahead and identify one potential challenge. Visualize how you might respond, focusing on remaining calm and exercising rational thought. In the evening, reflect on what transpired and express gratitude for the positives. When practiced regularly, this simple exercise can significantly enhance your emotional resilience and prepare you for whatever life may bring.

2.5 AMOR FATI: LOVING YOUR FATE AND FINDING JOY IN ADVERSITY

Imagine standing in a forest where the path forward is uncertain, and the road behind is a mosaic of joyous and challenging experiences. This is the essence of Amor Fati, a Stoic principle encouraging us to embrace our fate, love our life, and welcome both the sunshine and the storms with open arms. At its core, Amor Fati is about acceptance and love for one's life path, recognizing that every twist and turn has shaped who you are today. It's about seeing adversity not as an obstacle but as an opportunity for growth and harnessing the lessons embedded within each experience. When you adopt this mindset, you begin to appreciate the richness of life, understanding that every challenge is a stepping stone toward becoming a more resilient and compassionate individual.

Some of the most surprising research findings are that those who experienced significant life events, including major health diagnoses, are also the people who were able to accept their situation, notice the opportunities for growth, and thrive. Extensive research into post-traumatic growth underscores how trauma or adversity is often transformative in nature. Therefore, rather than being fearful of potential adversities, we should welcome the ups and downs of life for the opportunities that they provide. We have all endured our own hardships at some point in our lives. It is important to recognize the power of these in shaping us as individuals and reminding us of the importance of ups and downs in life for growth and transformation.

Practicing Amor Fati requires intentional reflection on your past experiences. Consider the moments that tested you, the trials that seemed insurmountable at the time. Reflect on what you learned from these episodes, how they transformed your perspective, and the strengths you gained. This reflection is not about dwelling on the past but acknowledging its role in your evolution. You could complement this practice with gratitude for your present circumstances. Each day, take a moment to express gratitude for the things you often overlook—a supportive friend, a warm meal, or even the breath that fills your lungs. By cultivating and pairing gratitude with Amor Fati, you become more attuned to the beauty amid life's chaos, nurturing a heart open to joy and contentment. For more information on cultivating gratitude, see Chapter 1 (1.5).

Embracing fate carries profound psychological and practical benefits. When you accept life as it is, you cultivate a sense of peace, freeing yourself from the shackles of regret and what-ifs. Regret is something that often holds many people back or has them pondering on what could have been. It is futile to ponder this when our past is no longer within our control. Our decisions have been made, the impact felt, and the opportunities for growth grasped. This acceptance fosters resilience, allowing you to adapt to change gracefully and confidently and leave regret behind. You become more adaptable and better equipped to handle life's unpredictability. By appreciating life's complexities and acknowledging that you have and will be able to get through the hardships, you develop a deeper understanding of yourself and the world around you, enriching your relationships and interactions with others. This mindset shift transforms how you approach daily challenges, encouraging you to find joy in the journey and celebrate each milestone.

Many have exemplified Amor Fati throughout history, finding strength and wisdom in acceptance. In his Stoic reflections, Marcus Aurelius often wrote about accepting one's destiny. He understood that life's unpredictability was part of its beauty, and by aligning with the natural order of things, he could navigate his responsibilities as an emperor with poise and integrity. His writings continue to inspire those seeking to live authentically and courageously.

In our contemporary world, countless individuals thrive through acceptance, embracing their unique paths with resilience and hope. Consider Christopher Reeve, the actor best known for portraying Superman, who developed paraplegia after a horse-riding accident in 1995. Instead of succumbing to despair, Reeve embraced his new reality and found purpose in advocacy. He became a leading voice for spinal cord injury research and disability rights, using his platform to inspire millions. Through his resilience, he demonstrated that even in the face of a life-altering situation, you can find meaning, strength, and a renewed sense of purpose. His story is a testament to loving one's fate—not merely accepting challenges but transforming them into a force for positive change.

Amor Fati invites you to view your life as a tapestry woven with threads of varying colors and textures. Each thread represents a moment in your journey, a story contributing to your life's vibrant masterpiece. By loving your fate, you honor the complexity of your existence, recognizing that even the darkest moments hold the potential for light. So, as you move forward, embrace each experience with an open heart, knowing that every step you take is part of a greater narrative, one filled with opportunities for learning, connection, and joy.

Reflection Activity: Amor Fati

Amor Fati, or "love of fate," is the Stoic practice of embracing all aspects of life—including challenges—as essential parts of our growth. Instead of resisting hardship, this mindset helps us see difficulties as opportunities to learn, adapt, and strengthen our character.

Step 1: Identify Challenges: Think of significant personal, professional, or emotional struggles you've faced. Write them down, noting the ones that shaped you most.

Step 2: Find the Lessons: For each challenge, consider what it taught you. Did it shift your perspective, uncover strengths you didn't know you had, or open new doors?

Step 3: Recognize Growth: Reflect on how these experiences changed you. Did they build resilience, patience, or wisdom? Who supported or influenced you during this time?

Difficult moments often make sense only in hindsight. The next time you encounter adversity, remind yourself that it may lead to growth, new opportunities, or deeper self-understanding. By accepting and even loving what happens, you empower yourself to move forward with strength and purpose.

2.6 THE INNER CITADEL: BUILDING YOUR MENTAL FORTRESS

Imagine your mind as a fortress, a secure haven that withstands the storms of life. This inner citadel is a metaphor for a resilient, self-fortified mind based on Stoic principles. In Stoic philosophy, mental fortitude is not just a desirable trait; it's a necessity. It empowers you to navigate life's unpredictability with strength and poise. Building resilience through inner strength fosters a steadfast mind that remains unshaken by external pressures or internal turmoil. Your inner citadel becomes a place of refuge where you find clarity and courage, no matter the circumstances.

Constructing this mental fortress involves intentional steps. By only engaging in a reflection activity once, you are committing to adding one brick to your mental fortress. However, we all know that more than one brick is needed to construct a fortress, and indeed, constant repairs, tweaks, and additions are needed to maintain it. Each practice, focused on emotion regulation, cultivating inner peace, building resilience, and accepting your fate, is critical for constructing a powerful fortress to guard yourself against emotional storms.

Begin with an initial self-reflection and introspection. How much of a fortress do you believe you have? Are these strategies already embedded into your daily routine? Do you actively try to improve your practice? After the initial reflection, use the below exercise to help you identify areas for improvement and develop a plan across the week to help you build some of these practices into your existing routine. At regular intervals, check in with yourself and review how your fortress is growing. Is it getting stronger or crumbling? Is there an area of weakness that needs more attention?

Protecting your inner fortress from external and internal threats requires vigilance. The world is filled with distractions, each vying for your attention and energy. To maintain focus, cultivate techniques that help you remain centered amidst chaos. Practice mindfulness, engage in purposeful activities, and set clear boundaries to guard your mental space.

Stories of resilience abound, offering inspiration for those building their inner citadels. Consider the Stoic philosopher Epictetus, who, despite being born into slavery, built a legacy of wisdom and strength. His teachings remind us that true freedom comes from within, unhindered by external conditions.

For a modern example, consider Viktor Frankl, a psychiatrist and Holocaust survivor who endured Auschwitz and other concentration camps during World War Two. Despite facing unimaginable suffering, Frankl found that the key to survival was one's ability to find meaning in suffering. In his seminal book, *Man's Search for Meaning*, Frankl recounts how those who maintained a sense of purpose—whether through love, faith, or a future goal—were more likely to endure hardship. He famously stated, *"Everything can be taken from a man but one thing: the last of the human freedoms—to choose one's attitude in any given set of circumstances, to choose one's own way."*

This perspective mirrors Epictetus's Stoic teachings, which emphasize that while external conditions may be beyond our control, our internal state—our thoughts, interpretations, and choices—remains our own. Frankl's ability to maintain inner freedom in Auschwitz exemplifies the ultimate application of Stoic philosophy in real-world adversity.

As you fortify your inner fortress, remember that this process is ongoing. Life's challenges will test your defenses, but each trial offers an opportunity to strengthen your mental fortress. Embrace these moments with courage and patience, knowing each step forward is a testament to your growth. With each stone you lay, your inner fortress becomes a beacon of strength, guiding you through the complexities of life with unwavering resolve. Armed with this resilience, you are prepared to face whatever lies ahead, confident in the knowledge that within you lies a sanctuary of strength and wisdom.

Practical Activity: Building Your Mental Fortress

Strengthening mental resilience requires consistent effort, much like building a physical fortress. This exercise will help you assess, implement, and refine practices that enhance your emotional and mental strength.

Step 1: Assess Your Resilience

Reflect on your current mental resilience. Do you handle stress well? Stay grounded in your values. Recognize areas where you can grow.

Step 2: Identify Key Strategies

Consider resilience-building techniques such as mindfulness, self-reflection, or emotional regulation. Which practices resonate most with you? Which could fit into your daily life?

Step 3: Integrate Small, Consistent Actions

Incorporate simple practices into your routine, such as a mindful morning walk, reflective journaling, or deep breathing exercises during breaks. Even 5-10 minutes daily can create lasting change.

Step 4: Reflect & Adjust Weekly

At the end of each week, review your progress. What worked well? What felt forced? Adjust your approach to fit your lifestyle while maintaining consistency.

By committing to regular mental training, you'll build a strong inner foundation—one that supports you in both calm and challenging times. Resilience is a lifelong practice strengthened through small, intentional actions.

In this chapter, we have explored how Stoic practices cultivate emotional intelligence, resilience, and inner calm. By embracing fate and building mental fortitude, you strengthen your ability to navigate challenges. The next chapter offers practical ways to apply Stoicism in daily life, equipping you to thrive. However, before moving on, use the below quote for your final reflection.

> *"A gem cannot be polished without friction, nor a man perfected without trials."*
>
> — SENECA, LETTERS TO LUCILIUS

3
INTEGRATING STOICISM INTO DAILY LIFE

"Waste no more time arguing what a good man should be. Be one."

— MARCUS AURELIUS

Integrating Stoicism into daily life, rather than as a one-time event, is key to building true resilience and wisdom. Life constantly presents challenges, and applying Stoic principles—focusing on what we can control, practicing gratitude, and embracing adversity—strengthens our ability to face difficulties with composure. Just as physical fitness requires regular exercise, mental fortitude develops through repeated practice. By making Stoicism a habit, we cultivate a stable, rational mindset that allows us to navigate uncertainty with clarity, purpose, and inner peace.

3.1 LIVING YOUR LIFE YOUR WAY: PERSONAL VALUES

At its cornerstone, Stoicism is grounded in the importance of values. These values are not the same as the four virtues discussed earlier but are values that you have decided for yourself. Everyone has their own set, and these are shaped by our histories, lives, and inner wants or desires. It is critical to use Stoicism in our daily lives so that we are clear about the values that we want to live by. You may already have your own set of defined values, or you may never have considered them before. However, it is essential to take the time before reading on to complete the exercise below to identify these.

Practical Activity: Identifying Your Core Values

Purpose: This exercise will help you define the values that guide your actions and decisions.

Step 1: Reflect on What Matters

Think about moments in your life when you felt proud, fulfilled, or at peace. These experiences can reveal what truly matters to you.

Step 2: Choose Your Core Values

Review the list below, or write down any that come to mind for you, and pick 3–5 values that resonate most with you:

1. **Integrity** – Doing the right thing, even when no one is watching
2. **Courage** – Facing challenges with strength and determination
3. **Wisdom** – Seeking truth, knowledge, and personal growth
4. **Discipline** – Staying committed to your goals and responsibilities
5. **Compassion** – Treating others with kindness and understanding

6. **Humility** – Recognizing your limits and remaining open to learning
7. **Gratitude** – Appreciating what you have and focusing on the present
8. **Resilience** – Bouncing back from setbacks with a positive mindset
9. **Simplicity** – Focusing on what truly matters and avoiding distractions
10. **Authenticity** – Living in alignment with your true self and beliefs
11. **Justice** – Striving to be fair and do what is right
12. **Patience** – Remaining calm and thoughtful in all situations
13. **Self-Reliance** – Trusting yourself and taking responsibility for your life
14. **Generosity** – Giving time, resources, and kindness freely
15. **Honesty** – Speaking truthfully and acting transparently
16. **Fortitude** – Enduring hardship with strength and grace
17. **Mindfulness** – Being present and aware in each moment
18. **Perseverance** – Staying dedicated despite obstacles
19. **Loyalty** – Being committed to your principles and those you care about
20. **Open-Mindedness** – Embracing new perspectives and continuous learning

Step 3: Apply Your Values to Daily Life

For each value you choose, ask yourself:

- How can I practice this value daily?
- What challenges might test my commitment to it?
- What is one small action I can take this week to embody this value?

By integrating these values into your daily life, you align your actions with Stoic principles and build a stronger sense of purpose.

3.2 STARTING YOUR DAY WITH A STOIC MINDSET: MORNING RITUALS

Picture this: a morning when you rise with the sun, the world outside still wrapped in the gentle embrace of dawn's quiet. The air is crisp, carrying a sense of promise. You pour yourself a cup of coffee, the steam curling upward like an invitation to pause, reflect, and set yourself up for success. In this serene moment, you are not just beginning another day; you are setting the stage for a life imbued with the wisdom of the Stoics. This practice is not merely about rituals but about cultivating a mindset that weaves Stoic principles seamlessly into the fabric of your daily existence.

Designing a morning routine with Stoicism is about more than just checking off a list of tasks. It's about creating a sacred space to ground yourself in the values that matter most. In Chapter 2, we discussed developing morning reflection activities. To extend this, consider incorporating Stoic affirmations into this ritual. It will add one minute to your practice, but the benefits over time compound significantly. Affirmations are not empty platitudes but powerful reminders of the virtues you aspire to embody—wisdom, courage, justice, and temperance alongside your life values. Repeat to yourself a phrase that resonates, perhaps, "I will meet today with patience and strength," allowing these words to infuse your spirit with purpose and resolve.

If affirmations are not something you are comfortable with yet, setting intentions aligned with Stoic virtues or values is another alternative to add to your morning routine. These intentions can become a compass for your day. Take a moment to reflect on what you wish to achieve, not in terms of tasks but personal growth. What virtues do you want to cultivate today? How can you embody wisdom in your decisions or courage in your actions? This intention-setting is not about perfection but progress, guiding you gently toward the person you wish to become. As you do this, you are not alone; you stand on the shoulders of giants - those philosophers who have pondered the same questions and found solace in pursuing virtue.

Affirmations and intention-setting are pivotal in anchoring your day in Stoic thought. As mentioned previously, they will only add around one minute to your existing morning routine or can be incorporated at any point in your day. These affirmations or daily intentions serve as a touchstone, a reminder to return to throughout the day when challenges arise. Use the below exercise to help to kickstart this process of integration into your daily reflections.

Reflection Activity: Crafting Your Affirmations

Purpose: These exercises will help you reinforce your values, build a strong mindset, and align your daily actions with what truly matters to you.

Step 1: Choose a Value

From the list of 20 values, select one that you want to focus on.

Step 2: Create a Personalized Affirmation

Use the following structure to craft your affirmation:

“I am [value], and I show it by [action].”

“I choose [value] in all situations, even when it’s difficult.”

“Every day, I grow stronger in my commitment to [value].”

Examples:

- “I am resilient, and I show it by embracing challenges as opportunities.”
- “I choose patience in all situations, even when I feel frustrated.”
- “Every day, I grow stronger in my commitment to honesty.”

Step 3: Repeat Your Affirmation Daily

- Say it aloud in the morning or before a challenge.
- Write it in a journal.
- Place it where you'll see it often (mirror, phone wallpaper, desk).

Reflection Activity: Setting Stoic Intentions

Intentions shape the way we approach each day. Unlike goals (which are outcome-driven), intentions focus on *how* you want to act and *who* you want to be.

Step 1: Pick a Value

Choose a value from the list that you'd like to embody more in your daily life.

Step 2: Set an Intention for the Day

Use these structures to create a meaningful intention:

"Today, I will practice [value] by [specific action]."

"I intend to embody [value] in my interactions and decisions today."

"No matter what happens, I will approach my day with [value]."

Examples:

- "Today, I will practice gratitude by acknowledging the small joys in my life."
- "I intend to embody integrity by speaking and acting with honesty."
- "No matter what happens, I will approach my day with resilience and inner strength."

Step 3: Reflect on Your Intention

At the end of the day, ask yourself:

- Did I act in alignment with my intention?
- How did this intention shape my actions or mindset?
- What will I focus on tomorrow?

3.3 MEDITATIVE MOMENTS: PRACTICING STOIC MEDITATION

In the fast-paced rhythm of our daily lives, meditation offers a pause —a moment to reconnect with ourselves. Stoic meditation, however, distinguishes itself by focusing on rational thought and emotional regulation. Where general mindfulness may center on presence, and we have explored this as a tool for emotional regulation, Stoic meditation emphasizes clarity and purpose, directing our minds toward understanding and integrating philosophical concepts into our lives. Stoic meditation, therefore, invites you to engage deeply with Stoic teachings, allowing them to shape your responses and attitudes. It's about finding equilibrium, confronting life's uncertainties calmly, and nurturing an inner dialogue that guides you toward wisdom and resilience.

To practice Stoic meditation, create a quiet, distraction-free space for contemplation. Light a candle or place a meaningful object nearby to anchor your thoughts. Choose a Stoic quote or concept to focus on, such as Marcus Aurelius's: *"You have power over your mind—not outside events. Realize this, and you will find strength."* Let the words sink in, repeating them softly in your mind. Reflect on their meaning and how they relate to your experiences and challenges. To make this a habit, select different Stoic quotes to meditate on daily or weekly. For more examples, see the activity below.

Reflection is a key part of Stoic meditation. As you meditate, thoughts may surface, connecting the concept to your own experiences. Afterward, take a moment to apply these insights to personal challenges. If you reflect on controlling your mind, consider the times when you gave too much power to external circumstances. How can you reclaim that power by focusing on your thoughts and actions? Whether brief or in-depth, this reflection bridges the gap between philosophy and practice, helping you live in alignment with Stoic ideals.

Regular Stoic meditation cultivates long-term benefits permeating every aspect of life. Remember that Stoic meditation differs from mindfulness or reflecting on the present moment due to its focus on overcoming challenges and contemplating adopting Stoic principles in our lives. Ensure you meditate on a phrase, quote, or idea and then record your response following it. Over time, you'll notice an enhanced emotional resilience, an ability to detach from negative emotions that previously held sway over your reactions. This resilience is not about suppressing feelings but recognizing them without being dominated by them. Improved emotional regulation allows you to respond to life's challenges with a steady mind, reducing the volatility of unchecked emotions. It's about cultivating a space within which clarity prevails, empowering you to face each day with renewed strength and purpose.

Incorporating Stoic meditation into your daily life is not merely a practice but a way of living. It invites you to engage with the world from a place of strength and understanding to cultivate a mindset that sees challenges as opportunities for growth. As you embrace this practice, you transform your inner world and how you interact with the world around you, fostering a life of resilience, wisdom, and profound peace.

Practical Activity: Stoic Meditation

To practice Stoic meditation, begin by creating a serene environment free from distractions. Choose a quiet space, perhaps lighting a candle or placing a meaningful object nearby to anchor your thoughts. Once settled, select a Stoic quote to focus on. Here are six options, but there are many freely available:

1. **"You have power over your mind—not outside events. Realize this, and you will find strength."** — *Marcus Aurelius*
2. **"The happiness of your life depends upon the quality of your thoughts."** — *Marcus Aurelius*
3. **"Difficulties strengthen the mind, as labor does the body."** — *Seneca*
4. **"Make the best use of what is in your power, and take the rest as it happens."** — *Epictetus*
5. **"Be tolerant with others and strict with yourself."** — *Marcus Aurelius*
6. **"Caretake this moment. Immerse yourself in its particulars."** — *Epictetus.*

As you meditate, repeat the chosen quote softly in your mind, allowing its meaning to unfold. Reflect on how it relates to your current experiences and challenges. To integrate this practice into your routine, consider focusing on a different quote each day or week, deepening your understanding and application of Stoic principles over time.

3.4 STOIC JOURNALING: DAILY REFLECTIONS FOR GROWTH

Reflection has been a critical component of the exercises so far. However, for many of us, reflecting in our minds alone is tricky. Significant benefits have been found in the practice of journaling, and today, this approach has been adopted by modern schools of thought. Writing thoughts down helps bring clarity and is a key Stoic practice adopted by many Stoic philosophers to make sense of their experiences and insights.

Imagine opening a blank page, pen in hand, ready to explore the depths of your inner world. This moment is where Stoic journaling begins, a practice rooted deeply in self-examination and personal growth. Stoic journaling isn't simply about recounting the day's events; it's a deliberate reflection that allows you to engage with your virtues and actions. Each entry becomes a mirror, reflecting your achievements and areas where improvement is necessary. Through this practice, you embark on a path of self-improvement, where writing becomes a tool for cultivating wisdom and clarity. Journaling enables you to step back from the noise of everyday life and consider how your actions align with the principles you strive to embody. It allows you to complete your daily reflection but in a more structured way, using a method that will enable you to review weeks or months of previous reflections.

A well-structured Stoic journal entry can transform this reflective practice into a powerful daily ritual. Start your day with morning prompts that set the tone. Consider questions like, *"What is within my control today?"* or *"Which virtues will guide my actions?"* These prompts encourage you to focus on what truly matters, helping you approach the day with intention and purpose. Use evening reflections to assess your actions against Stoic values as the day concludes. Reflect on moments where you responded to challenges with virtue, and identify areas where you can grow. This dual approach—morning intention-setting through journaling and evening reflection—creates a balanced routine that strengthens your commitment to living virtuously. For more information on intention-setting, review Activity 3.2 in Chapter 3.

To deepen your journaling practice, consider incorporating specific prompts that encourage thorough reflection. Questions such as "How did I respond to challenges with virtue?" or "What opportunities did I seize to practice patience?" invite you to engage with your experiences critically and constructively. By examining these moments, you gain insight into your habitual patterns, understanding what drives you and where you might be holding back. This self-awareness catalyzes change, empowering you to make decisions that align more closely with your values. As you engage with these prompts regularly, you cultivate a habit of introspection that enhances your capacity for personal growth.

The benefits of consistent journaling extend far beyond the pages of your notebook. As you commit to this practice, you'll notice increased self-awareness and emotional intelligence. You'll become more attuned to your thoughts and feelings and better equipped to navigate the complexities of your inner world. This heightened awareness fosters clarity in personal and professional decision-making as you learn to recognize the motivations behind your actions and their alignment with your values. Regular journaling reinforces Stoic principles in your daily life, helping you to cultivate a mindset that embraces resilience, adaptability, and growth.

Practical Activity: Journaling For Impact

Set aside a few minutes each morning and evening for Stoic journaling. Remember that this can build into the reflection practice that you have cultivated in the previous chapters. However, rather than keeping reflections in your head, write them down to deepen your awareness. Use prompts to explore your thoughts freely, focusing on how your actions align with your values. This practice isn't about perfection but progress, an opportunity to connect with yourself, gain insight, and cultivate personal growth. Over time, journaling becomes a foundation for a life guided by wisdom and continuous evolution.

3.5 HANDLING EVERYDAY IRRITATIONS: TRAFFIC, QUEUES, AND MORE

In the midst of our bustling lives, it's often the tiny irritations, like being stuck in traffic, waiting in long queues, or dealing with minor inconveniences, that test our patience and composure. These moments, though seemingly trivial, provide fertile ground for applying Stoic principles. By recognizing triggers and practicing detachment, you can transform these daily annoyances into opportunities for growth. Consider the frustration of a traffic jam. Instead of succumbing to impatience, use this time to practice deep breathing. Inhale slowly and deeply, then exhale, releasing tension with each breath. This not only calms your nerves but also helps you detach from the situation, allowing you to observe it without emotional upheaval.

Additionally, this is where the dichotomy of control is of significance. Remember that we often focus on what we cannot control. Pause and think to yourself: is this something that I can control? If it isn't, there is no point in wasting time and energy on it, potentially setting yourself up for an emotional chain reaction in your body that could have been completely avoided.

Reframing situations as opportunities for virtue is another powerful Stoic technique. When faced with a long queue at the grocery store, for example, shift your perspective. Instead of viewing the wait as wasted time, see it as a chance to practice patience or engage in reflection. Engage with those around you, striking up a conversation or offering a smile. These small acts of kindness not only make the wait more pleasant but also strengthen your capacity for empathy. By reframing these moments, you cultivate a mindset that seeks the positive in every situation, turning potential frustrations into meaningful experiences.

Practical examples of Stoic responses can be your guide in navigating everyday irritations. Imagine you're at a crowded coffee shop, and the line seems endless. Rather than allowing impatience to take hold, focus on observing your surroundings. Notice the details you might otherwise overlook, such as the warmth of the café and the aroma of freshly brewed coffee. This mindfulness anchors you in the present, transforming what could be a moment of irritation into one of appreciation. Similarly, when dealing with an unexpected delay, take it as an opportunity for reflection. Use the time to ponder a Stoic quote or reflect on your day, finding wisdom in the pause.

Mastering minor irritations has a profound impact on your overall well-being. As you learn to navigate these challenges with equanimity, you'll notice a reduction in stress and an increase in daily satisfaction. By not allowing minor frustrations to dominate your mood, you free up mental energy for more meaningful activities. This greater focus enhances your ability to engage with the tasks and people that matter most, enriching your life in countless ways. The skills you develop in managing minor annoyances extend to more significant challenges, fortifying your emotional resilience and empowering you to face life's complexities with confidence and grace.

Practical Activity: Reframing Daily Irritations

Minor frustrations are inevitable, but how we respond to them shapes our emotional well-being. This exercise helps you shift perspective and cultivate patience.

Step 1: Identify Daily Irritations

List small, recurring annoyances—traffic, long lines, slow service, or delays. What tends to disrupt your mood?

Step 2: Reframe Your Thinking

For each irritation, ask:

- Is this within my control? If not, practice acceptance.
- Will this matter in a few hours or days? Gain perspective.
- How can I turn this into something positive?

Examples:

- **Traffic jam:** Use the time to listen to a podcast or practice deep breathing.

- **Slow service:** Take a moment to observe your surroundings and enjoy the pause.

Step 3: Implement & Reflect

At the end of the day, ask yourself:

- Did I react with patience or frustration?
- Did my new approach improve my mood?
- What can I refine for next time?

By consistently reframing irritations, you train yourself to remain calm in the face of minor stressors, strengthening emotional resilience for bigger challenges.

As we move on to the next chapter to explore how stoicism can improve our decision-making, use this quote for your final reflection.

> *"You have power over your mind—not outside events. Realize this, and you will find strength."*
>
> — MARCUS AURELIUS, MEDITATIONS

4
ENHANCING DECISION-MAKING WITH STOICISM

"Hesitation is the death of action, and delay will be the undoing of us."

— SENECA, LETTERS TO LUCILIUS

Imagine standing at a crossroads, confronted with a decision that could change the course of your life. The weight of choice hangs heavy, and the path forward seems obscured by a fog of uncertainty and emotion. In moments like these, the teachings of Stoicism offer a beacon of clarity, guiding you through the haze with the light of reason. Stoicism is an ancient philosophy that champions rationality and virtue, providing the tools to navigate decisions with confidence and composure. Its focus on clear, logical thinking empowers you to make choices rooted in wisdom rather than emotion, ensuring your decisions align with your values and aspirations.

4.1 IMPROVING DECISION-MAKING: APPLYING RATIONAL THOUGHT

At the heart of Stoic decision-making is the emphasis on using reason over emotion. This approach encourages you to evaluate your choices through a rational lens, filtering out the noise of impulsive feelings that might cloud your judgment. By prioritizing logic, you can discern the essence of the decision at hand, separating facts from fleeting sentiments. This rational foundation serves as a sturdy platform from which you can assess your options objectively, avoiding the pitfalls of rash choices driven by temporary emotions. The Stoics believed that by cultivating this mindset, you could achieve a sense of tranquility and confidence, knowing that your decisions are guided by the principles of truth and virtue.

This approach does not dismiss emotions but instead organizes them, allowing you to observe and evaluate them without feeling pressured to react impulsively. Emotions serve as signals, not commands demanding immediate action. By acknowledging them without being ruled by them, you gain clarity. For example, if you feel fear when facing a significant life decision, recognize it as a natural response. Name the emotion, separate it from the situation, evaluate its validity, and then proceed with a rational assessment of the pros and cons. This process enables you to make clear, thoughtful decisions rather than being swayed by fleeting feelings.

To enhance clarity in decision-making, break complex choices into manageable parts. This approach reduces overwhelm and provides a clearer perspective. By dissecting the problem, you can identify core issues and address them systematically. Logical frameworks, such as pros and cons lists, help evaluate options by weighing short- and long-term outcomes. This structured process clarifies thinking and boosts confidence, ensuring decisions are based on thorough analysis. Writing pros and cons down can be especially powerful, offering a visual guide to the best path forward.

In practice, rational decision-making can be applied across various facets of life. Consider a career decision where you're weighing the prospect of a new job against your current position. By analyzing the pros and cons of each option, you can objectively assess factors such as job satisfaction, growth opportunities, and work-life balance. This rational evaluation helps illuminate the choice that best aligns with your long-term goals and values. Similarly, in personal relationships, applying logical reasoning can clarify your actions and responses. For instance, when faced with a conflict, stepping back to consider the situation calmly allows you to respond thoughtfully rather than react impulsively. This approach fosters healthier, more constructive interactions.

The benefits of making decisions based on clarity and logic are manifold. First and foremost, this approach enhances your confidence in your choices. When you know that your decision is grounded in reason and thorough analysis, you can proceed with assurance, free from the nagging doubts that often accompany impulsive choices. This confidence reduces the likelihood of regret and second-guessing as you've considered the implications of your decision carefully. Moreover, rational decision-making aligns your actions with your values, ensuring that your choices contribute to a fulfilling and meaningful life. This alignment fosters a sense of integrity and purpose, empowering you to navigate life's crossroads with grace and wisdom.

Practical Activity: Making Decisions with Clarity and Logic

Purpose: This exercise helps you separate emotions from decision-making, evaluate choices rationally, and gain confidence in your decisions.

Step 1: Identify a Recent Decision

Think of a decision—big or small—that left you feeling uncertain. It could be a career move, a relationship choice, or an everyday dilemma where emotions clouded your judgment.

Step 2: Break It Down

Ask yourself:

- **Emotional Influence:** What emotions were at play? Were you driven by fear, excitement, pressure, or habit?
- **Logical Perspective:** What are the facts? What rational considerations support or challenge this choice?
- **Short-Term vs. Long-Term Pros & Cons:**
    - *Short-Term:* How will this decision affect you immediately? Will it bring relief, stress, or convenience?
    - *Long-Term:* How does this choice align with your values and goals? Will it create stability, growth, or unintended consequences?
- **Perspective Shift:** If you were advising a friend, what would you tell them?

Step 3: Apply This to Future Decisions

When facing a tough choice, pause and walk through this reflection. Separating emotions from logic helps you make clearer, more intentional decisions that align with your long-term well-being.

4.2 OVERCOMING FEAR AND DOUBT: TRUSTING STOIC WISDOM

Fear and doubt are familiar companions on the path of decision-making. They lurk in the shadows, whispering uncertainties that can paralyze us. Fear of failure often looms large, casting a long shadow over our choices. The worry of making the wrong decision can hinder our ability to act, trapping us in a cycle of indecision. Doubt in our abilities compounds this fear, eroding confidence and amplifying hesitations. These emotions, left unchecked, can stifle progress and prevent us from seizing opportunities. Yet, Stoicism offers a framework to confront these feelings, transforming them from roadblocks into stepping stones.

Stoic teachings guide us to see fear as transient, a fleeting emotion that need not dictate our actions. By recognizing that fear is often exaggerated by our minds, we can diminish its power over us. The Stoics remind us that while fear is a natural response, it doesn't have to be the driving force behind our decisions. Instead, the dichotomy of control comes into play, and we are encouraged to focus on what we can control—our emotional reactions, thoughts, and actions. This shift in perspective fosters self-confidence, allowing us to approach decisions with a calm, rational mindset. By aligning our choices with virtues such as courage and wisdom, we build a foundation of trust in ourselves.

Consider a significant decision you've made—or hesitated to make. Why does the fear of failure hold you back? Often, it's not failure itself, but the fear of not succeeding that keeps us stuck. How many things have you wanted to try but never started because of this fear?

Pause and reflect: Why does failure matter? Maybe it's the fear of others seeing you fail. But remember, we cannot control what others think or feel. Let that sink in. We fear failure because we worry about perception, yet most people are too focused on their own lives to dwell on ours.

By allowing this fear to stop us, we avoid pursuing what we truly want based on an external factor we can never control. Instead, shift your focus to what is within your control—your thoughts, actions, and emotional responses. When you direct your energy here, you unlock an inner strength that frees you to take bold steps toward your goals.

Throughout history, individuals have drawn on Stoicism to overcome fear and doubt. Consider the Roman emperor Marcus Aurelius, who faced the immense pressures of leadership amidst political turmoil. His writings reveal a man who, despite his fears, trusted in

Stoic principles to guide his decisions. By focusing on what lay within his control, Marcus found clarity and strength. In modern times, leaders across various fields have embraced these teachings. Take a business executive who must navigate a volatile market. By applying Stoic wisdom, they remain grounded, focusing on strategy rather than succumbing to panic. This success illustrates the enduring power of Stoic teachings.

A modern example is Tim Cook, the CEO of Apple. When he took over after Steve Jobs, many doubted his ability to lead the company to continued success. This fear and doubt could have overwhelmed him when needing to live up to his predecessor. Rather than worrying about external opinions or trying to imitate Jobs, Cook remained focused on what he could control—making thoughtful, strategic decisions, maintaining Apple's culture of innovation, and leading with integrity. By prioritizing rational action over fear or public perception, he solidified Apple's position as one of the leading companies in the world. His approach reflects Stoic principles: focusing on strategy, ignoring external noise, and staying committed to personal and professional values.

While fear and doubt may never entirely disappear, they need not control your life. They are a natural part of the process, a signal that you are making a big, often life-changing decision; they are not something to shrink away from. By trusting in Stoic wisdom and focusing on the elements within your control, you can navigate your decisions with greater certainty and peace.

Reflection Activity: Understanding Fear and Taking Control

Purpose: Break down fears, focus on what you can control, and develop a plan to take action.

Step 1: Identify Your Fear

Write down a fear or anxiety holding you back. Be as detailed as possible.

Step 2: Shift Focus to Control

- What aspects of this fear can you influence? (Your actions, preparation, mindset)
- What is beyond your control? (External events, others' reactions)

Step 3: Take Action

List 2-3 concrete steps to strengthen your confidence and handle the situation proactively.

Step 4: Release What You Can't Control

Ask yourself: *Is worrying about this helping me?* Accept uncertainty instead of resisting it. Use a simple mantra:

"I focus on what I can control and release what I cannot."

Step 5: Reflect

After a few days, revisit your approach. Has shifting focus reduced your anxiety? What worked, and what can you improve?

By consistently applying this exercise, you train yourself to approach fears rationally, reducing anxiety and building resilience in the face of challenges.

4.3 BALANCING CONTROL AND ACCEPTANCE IN DECISION-MAKING

In life's complexities, Stoicism offers a balance between control and acceptance. While you can influence some aspects of life, many remain beyond your reach. The dichotomy of control isn't just about making decisions—it's about embracing outcomes beyond your control. Imagine starting a business. You can plan strategically, anticipate challenges, and set goals, yet market shifts, new competitors, or changing consumer preferences may still shape the outcome.

Stoicism encourages you to accept uncertainty as part of the process —focus on your efforts and make peace with the results, whatever they may be.

To maintain this balance, you need to develop strategies that integrate both control and acceptance. Begin by setting realistic expectations for the outcomes of your decisions. This involves acknowledging the factors you can influence and those you cannot. By doing so, you prepare yourself for a range of possible scenarios, reducing the shock of unexpected results. Acceptance of the uncontrollable aspects is equally crucial. This practice doesn't mean resignation but rather understanding that some elements lie outside your sphere of influence. By accepting these, you free yourself from the burden of trying to control the uncontrollable, allowing you to dedicate your energy to what truly matters.

This balanced approach to decision-making brings profound psychological benefits. It reduces anxiety over outcomes, as you're not constantly battling against the tide of uncertainty. Instead, you cultivate a greater sense of peace, knowing that you've done your part and that some things are simply beyond your control. This peace of mind allows you to remain focused and composed in complex situations, providing clarity and strength even when outcomes aren't as expected. By practicing this balance, you develop resilience, learning to adapt and thrive amidst life's unpredictability.

Balancing control and acceptance requires a shift in mindset, one that prioritizes effort over results. It involves letting go of the illusion of total control and embracing the fluidity of life. This mindset fosters adaptability, enabling you to respond to challenges with calm assurance. As you navigate decisions, remember that your power lies in how you choose to act and react. Embrace the unpredictability with an open heart, knowing that every outcome, whether anticipated or not, is an opportunity for growth and learning. This balance, though delicate, transforms how you engage with the world, empowering you to make decisions with both intention and acceptance.

Practical Activity: Balancing Control and Acceptance in Decision-Making

Purpose: This exercise helps you evaluate a decision, focus on what you can control, and accept uncertainties with confidence.

Step 1: Define Your Decision

Clearly state the decision you're facing (e.g., applying for a job in a new city).

Step 2: Identify Steps You've Taken

List the actions you've taken (or plan to take) to improve the outcome. For example, researching opportunities, updating your resume, and assessing financial feasibility.

Step 3: Consider Possible Outcomes

Think through different scenarios:

- *Best case:* Things work out well, and you thrive.
- *Likely outcomes:* You succeed but face initial challenges.
- *Worst case:* Things don't go as planned, and you feel disappointed.

Step 4: Prepare for Challenges

Identify potential difficulties and how to handle them:

- If stress is a concern, create a detailed plan to manage tasks.
- If rejection is a possibility, focus on improving your skills and applying elsewhere.
- If loneliness is a factor, research social groups or support networks in advance.

Step 5: Reframe & Adjust

Ask yourself:

- Have I done everything reasonably within my control?
- Am I accepting uncertainty rather than resisting it?
- Would adjusting my expectations or timeline make this decision easier?

Write any final thoughts or insights gained from this exercise, such as: *"I realize that even if the worst-case scenario happens, I can handle it by taking alternative steps. I feel more confident moving forward."*

This activity helps you shift focus from anxiety over uncertainty to practical preparation and acceptance. By balancing control and adaptability, you can navigate complex decisions with clarity, confidence, and resilience.

4.4 THE ROLE OF VIRTUES IN GUIDING CHOICES

In the tapestry of decision-making, Stoic virtues serve as the threads that weave together ethical and value-driven choices. At the heart of this philosophy lies the belief that virtues like wisdom, courage, justice, and temperance are not mere ideals but practical guides that inform our actions and decisions. Wisdom, for instance, acts as a compass, helping you see the broader implications of your choices. It encourages a deep understanding of the context and consequences, preventing you from being swayed by fleeting emotions or short-term gains. Wisdom illuminates the path, allowing you to make informed decisions that align with both your personal goals and the greater good.

Courage, on the other hand, empowers you to make decisions that may be difficult but necessary. It is the strength to stand firm in your convictions even when faced with uncertainty or opposition. Courage propels you to act in accordance with your values, especially when the stakes are high. Whether it's speaking up against injustice or making a life-changing decision that defies convention, courage ensures that your choices are not only bold but also grounded in integrity. These virtues, when embraced, transform decision-making from a mere mechanical process into a meaningful expression of your character and principles.

Integrating virtues into your decision-making process begins with reflection. Before making a final choice, pause to consider how it aligns with your values. Ask yourself which virtues are at play and how they can guide you. This virtue-based reflection helps clarify your intentions, ensuring that your actions resonate with your ethical beliefs. Aligning your decisions with personal and ethical values requires a conscious effort to prioritize what truly matters to you. When faced with a dilemma, consider how each option reflects your commitment to virtues like honesty, fairness, and compassion. This alignment acts as a filter, allowing you to sift through the noise and focus on what is genuinely important.

Consider a parent who receives a job offer in a new city 3,000 miles away. If they based their decision solely on salary, it might seem like an obvious choice. However, upon deeper reflection, they recognize that their core values, family, and close friendships are essential to their happiness and way of life. If they focused only on financial gain, they might overlook the trade-offs, such as reduced time with loved ones and the impact on their personal connections. By evaluating the decision holistically, they can ensure their choice aligns with what truly matters to them.

The long-term benefits of making decisions guided by Stoic virtues are profound. Such choices cultivate a reputation for integrity and trustworthiness as others recognize your commitment to ethical principles. This trust becomes the foundation of lasting relationships, both personal and professional. Moreover, acting in accordance with your values enhances your self-respect and fulfillment. When your decisions resonate with your core beliefs, you experience a sense of alignment and harmony, knowing that you are living authentically. This alignment not only enriches your own life but also inspires those around you, creating a ripple effect of positive change and ethical awareness.

Practical Activity: Making Decisions with Virtue and Clarity

Purpose: This exercise helps you evaluate a decision through the lens of Stoic virtues to ensure it aligns with wisdom, courage, justice, temperance, and your personal values.

Step 1: Identify Your Decision

Write down a decision you are facing (e.g., downsizing your home after your children have moved out).

Step 2: Evaluate Through the Virtues

Reflect on the following:

- **Wisdom:** What are the long-term implications? Will this choice improve or complicate your life?
- **Courage:** Does fear or emotional attachment hold you back? What discomfort must you face?
- **Justice:** How does this impact others? Are you balancing your needs with those of loved ones?
- **Temperance:** Does this decision create balance, or does it lean too much toward comfort or loss?
- **Personal Values:** Does this choice align with what truly matters to you?

Step 3: Analyze & Adjust

- Is your decision well-balanced across these virtues, or is it driven by one more than the others?
- Would any adjustments help align your choice with wisdom, courage, justice, or temperance?

- Does this decision reflect or contradict your core values?

Step 4: Apply & Reflect

Revisit this framework as you move forward to ensure your decision stays aligned with your virtues and values. If challenges arise, use this approach to reassess and adjust.

By integrating Stoic virtues into decision-making, you build clarity, integrity, and resilience, ensuring choices that lead to long-term fulfillment.

4.5 LEARNING FROM MISTAKES: A STOIC APPROACH TO FAILURE

Mistakes are an inevitable part of the human experience, and within the Stoic framework, they are not only acknowledged but also embraced as essential catalysts for growth. Errors, rather than being seen as failures, are perceived as valuable opportunities for learning and self-improvement. The Stoics taught that every misstep is a chance to refine our understanding and sharpen our skills. By viewing mistakes through this lens, you transform setbacks into stepping stones, guiding you toward a more enlightened path. This perspective fosters a mindset that welcomes challenges as integral to personal and professional development, turning adversity into a wellspring of wisdom.

Learning from past mistakes is essential for growth and better decision-making. Surprisingly, however, research indicates that learning from failure can be more challenging than commonly believed. A study from the University of Chicago found that people often learn less from failure than from success, possibly due to the negative emotions associated with failure leading individuals to disengage from the learning process. This is why structured reflection on failure is crucial. By actively analyzing mistakes, identifying lessons, considering alternatives, and adjusting future actions, you can turn setbacks into valuable learning experiences, improving both life satisfaction and decision-making.

One effective method for structured reflection is through active deconstructing exercises. This involves analyzing what went wrong, identifying lessons learned, and developing strategies to avoid similar errors in the future. By adopting this approach, individuals can transform setbacks into valuable learning experiences, ultimately enhancing life satisfaction and decision-making capabilities.

Stoicism emphasizes the development of resilience through failure by normalizing these experiences and encouraging a mindset shift. Encouraging this mindset shift helps you view each mistake as a valuable teacher, guiding you toward continuous learning and improvement.

Throughout history, numerous individuals have demonstrated the power of Stoic principles in overcoming failure. Thomas Edison, for instance, famously stated, "I have not failed. I've just found 10,000 ways that won't work," highlighting his unwavering commitment to perseverance. His story is a testament to the idea that failure is merely a stepping stone to success. On a more personal level, consider the everyday examples of resilience and recovery in those around you. From a friend who bounced back after a job loss to a family member who rebuilt their life following a personal setback, these stories inspire and affirm the transformative potential of embracing mistakes.

As you reflect on the role of mistakes in your life, remember that they are not to be feared but embraced as opportunities for growth. By reframing errors as valuable experiences, you cultivate a mindset that thrives on learning and adaptation. Through this lens, each misstep becomes a catalyst for resilience and success, empowering you to approach challenges with renewed vigor and insight.

Reflection Activity: Deconstructing Past Mistakes To Enable Growth

Mistakes are opportunities for learning and growth. Use this short exercise to reflect on a past mistake, extract valuable lessons, and strengthen your future decision-making.

Step 1: Identify the Mistake

- What happened?
- What was the outcome?

Step 2: Analyze What Went Wrong

- Which parts of the situation did not go as planned?
- Were there specific errors in your actions, decisions, or mindset?

Step 3: Consider Alternatives

- What could you have done differently?
- Were there warning signs or alternative choices you overlooked?

Step 4: Consider Your Values

- Did I act in accordance with my values?
- Were there opportunities to integrate my values, which were overlooked?

Step 5: Extract Key Lessons

- What insights have you gained from this experience?
- How can this mistake make you stronger or more prepared for the future?

Step 6: Plan for Future Success

- What actions will you take to prevent a similar mistake?
- What skills, habits, or strategies will you develop to improve your approach?

By shifting your mindset to see mistakes as learning experiences, you cultivate resilience and ensure that every setback becomes a stepping stone toward future success.

With these insights in mind, we now turn our focus to the next chapter, where we will explore the development of self-discipline and focus. These qualities, when combined with the wisdom gained from embracing mistakes, form the foundation for a life of intentionality and resilience. Before moving on, use the quote below for a final reflection.

> *"If you want to improve, be content to be thought foolish and stupid."*
>
> — EPICTETUS, ENCHIRIDION

MAKE A DIFFERENCE WITH YOUR REVIEW

Unlock the Power of Generosity

"A person's worth is measured by the good they do, not by what they have."
Marcus Aurelius

When we give without expecting anything in return, we not only help others, but we enrich our own lives. Would you help someone just like you—curious about Stoicism but unsure where to begin? My mission is to make Stoicism simple, practical, and accessible to all.

But to reach more people, I need your help.

Most people choose books based on reviews. Your words could be the reason someone discovers the power of Stoicism and applies it to their life. It costs nothing, takes less than a minute, and could change someone's journey. Your review could help...

- ...one more person find peace in chaos.
- ...one more reader gain the courage to face challenges.
- ...one more mind unlock the wisdom of ancient philosophy.
- ...one more life be transformed by the wisdom of Stoic principles.

To make a difference, simply scan the QR code below and leave a review:
If you love helping others, you're my kind of person. Thank you from the bottom of my heart!, Charlie Steele

https://www.amazon.com/dp/1068797738

5
DEVELOPING SELF-DISCIPLINE AND FOCUS

"No man is free who is not master of himself."

— EPICTETUS, DISCOURSES, 2.1

Imagine you're at a bustling market, surrounded by a myriad of sights and sounds, each vendor calling out to you with enticing offers. This market represents the myriad of temptations life presents us every day, those alluring distractions that pull your attention and sway your focus. In the midst of this chaos, self-control stands as your guiding compass, steering you toward your true north. In Stoicism, self-control is not an abstract ideal but a fundamental virtue vital for resisting short-term temptations in favor of long-term goals. It's about making rational choices that align with your deeper values rather than succumbing to fleeting impulses.

5.1 SELF-CONTROL AND TEMPTATIONS

The Stoic perspective on desires is clear: desires, when left unchecked, can distort your beliefs and compel irrational actions, leading to unnecessary suffering when they remain unfulfilled. Stoicism encourages you to align your desires with nature, urging you to accept what is within your control and release what is not. This alignment fosters a mindset where rational choice prevails over impulse, enabling you to navigate desires with clarity and purpose. By focusing on what you can influence, you cultivate a sense of peace and fulfillment, unburdened by the constant pursuit of transient pleasures.

Enhancing self-control requires practical strategies that you can apply in everyday situations. One effective technique is practicing delayed gratification. This involves consciously postponing immediate rewards to gain more significant benefits in the future. For instance, when faced with the temptation of an unhealthy snack, pause and remind yourself of your health goals. Visualize the long-term benefits of choosing a healthier option, and let this vision guide your decision. Research indicates that individuals who can delay gratification often experience better life outcomes, as it has been linked with improved well-being. For instance, research published in the *Journal of Happiness Studies* found that individuals who practice self-control and delay gratification report higher life satisfaction than those who do not.

Another strategy is identifying and managing triggers. Pay attention to the situations or emotions that prompt impulsive behavior. By recognizing these triggers, you can develop proactive responses that align with your values.

Everyday temptations test your self-control regularly, and learning to navigate them is crucial. Consider the allure of unhealthy food choices. You're at a dinner party, and the dessert table is laden with tempting treats. In this scenario, exercise self-control by focusing on your commitment to health. Remind yourself of the reasons behind your dietary choices and the satisfaction of achieving your health goals through positive visualization. Then, employ a distraction technique, shift your attention to the company and conversation, savoring the experience without compromising your values.

The benefits of mastering self-control extend far beyond resisting temptations. On a personal level, self-control empowers you to achieve your goals more effectively. You learn to prioritize tasks, manage time efficiently, and persevere in the face of challenges.

Take another example: procrastination in tasks is another frequent challenge. When faced with the urge to delay a task, many of us engage in the daily battle of putting tasks off or falling into the trap of procrastination, where we haven't made any progress. There are many prompts that we can use to help us overcome procrastination.

If a task feels overwhelming, break it down into smaller, manageable steps and write them out. Checking off each step provides a small dopamine boost, reinforcing progress and motivation. For longer tasks, use focused time intervals—such as 20-minute sessions—followed by short breaks to maintain momentum. If starting feels daunting, commit to just 2 minutes of work. Set a timer, count down from 10, and begin. Often, once you've started, you'll naturally continue beyond those 2 minutes, overcoming the initial resistance and building momentum.

This discipline translates into greater satisfaction and fulfillment as you realize your aspirations. Professionally, self-control enhances your reliability and trustworthiness. Colleagues and partners recognize your consistent commitment to excellence, fostering strong relationships built on trust. This reputation for dependability opens doors to new opportunities and collaborations, enhancing your career growth.

Reflection Activity: Your Self-Control Toolkit

Purpose: Identify areas where you struggle with self-control, recognize triggers, and develop strategies to stay aligned with your goals.

Step 1: Identify Your Challenge

What area do you struggle with? Choose one or more:

- **Diet & Eating Habits** – Unhealthy cravings, emotional eating, portion control.
- **Procrastination & Avoidance** – Delaying tasks, losing focus, wasting time.
- **Other Areas** – Shopping, social media, negative habits.

Example: *I snack late at night even when I'm not hungry.*

Step 2: Recognize Your Triggers

What causes your self-control struggles?

- **Emotional triggers:** Stress, boredom, and frustration.
- **Environmental triggers:** Easy access to temptations and digital distractions.
- **Habitual triggers:** Mindless snacking, avoiding tasks out of habit.

Example: *I snack while watching TV at night.*

Step 3: Develop a Strategy for Control

Create a plan to counteract triggers:

- **Diet & Eating:** Remove temptations, pause before eating, and set mealtime rules.
- **Procrastination:** Use the 2-minute rule, set time blocks, eliminate distractions, and reframe tasks.

Example: *Instead of snacking, I'll drink herbal tea and read before bed.*

Step 4: Build Your Self-Control Toolkit

Record the following:

- **My Challenge:** (What I struggle with)
- **My Triggers:** (What causes me to lose control)
- **My New Strategy:** (How I will regain control)

Example:

- *My Challenge:* Procrastination on work tasks.
- *My Triggers:* Checking my phone constantly.
- *My New Strategy:* Use 20-minute focus sessions with the phone on silent.

Step 5: Reflect & Adjust

After a week, ask: Did my strategy help? What worked? What needs adjusting?

By understanding your triggers and applying intentional strategies, you strengthen self-control, making it easier to stay on track with your long-term goals.

5.2 THE STOIC APPROACH TO GOAL SETTING AND ACHIEVEMENT

Imagine you are standing at the foot of a mountain, looking up at the peak you wish to conquer. This peak symbolizes your goals, which are lofty yet attainable with the right mindset and approach. In Stoicism, goal setting is a process deeply rooted in virtue and rationality. It's not just about reaching the summit but about ensuring that the path you take aligns with your personal values and ethics. A Stoic's journey to achieving goals isn't marked by impulsive leaps but by deliberate, reasoned steps that resonate with one's core beliefs. This alignment ensures that your goals are not just desires but reflections of who you are and what you stand for. When your objectives are infused with virtue, the journey becomes as meaningful as the destination.

Maintaining clarity and measurability is essential to set goals effectively. Begin by defining goals that are specific and actionable. Instead of a vague desire to "be healthier," articulate a clear objective like "walk 30 minutes daily for the next month." This specificity transforms abstract wishes into concrete plans. Regularly reviewing and adjusting these goals ensures they remain relevant and achievable. Life is dynamic, and as circumstances change, so should your goals. This adaptability allows you to stay true to your path while accommodating the ebbs and flows of life. Consistent reflection on your progress not only keeps you focused but also provides the motivation to persevere, even when the climb gets steep.

Challenges and setbacks are inevitable, but they need not deter you. When obstacles arise, draw upon Stoic strategies to maintain motivation and focus. Visualize your goals and the virtues they embody. This visualization serves as a reminder of your commitment, igniting the inner drive to push forward. When faced with failure, view it as a lesson rather than a defeat. Analyze what went wrong, such as through the exercise shared in Chapter 4 (4.5), adjust your course, and continue with newfound wisdom. This mindset not only cultivates resilience but transforms setbacks into valuable learning experiences. Each stumble becomes an opportunity to refine your approach, bringing you one step closer to your desired peak in a way that is manageable for you.

Real-life examples highlight the power of Stoic goal-setting. Take Kobe Bryant, whose *Mamba Mentality* embodied relentless self-discipline and mastery. In his book, *The Mamba Mentality: How I Play*, he details his meticulous approach—perfecting footwork, refining his shot, and studying opponents—through disciplined, daily practice.

His commitment extended beyond basketball, leading to success as a storyteller and entrepreneur.

Bryant's Stoic-like resilience shows that mastery isn't about talent alone but patience, persistence, and growth. Likewise, personal development thrives under Stoic principles. A lifelong learner mastering a new skill does so through small, consistent efforts. Over time, they not only gain expertise but also cultivate the discipline and patience essential for lasting success.

As you begin your journey toward achieving your goals, remember that the path is as significant as the destination. By setting goals grounded in virtue and rationality, you ensure that each step you take is meaningful and aligned with your true self. Embrace the challenges along the way as opportunities to learn and grow, and trust that with persistence and reflection, you will reach your summit.

Practical Activity: The Goal Setting Blueprint for Success

This exercise ensures clarity, preparation, and resilience in achieving your goal by anticipating obstacles and planning solutions.

Step 1: Define Your Goal

Choose a meaningful goal and be specific about what success looks like.

Example: *Run a 5K race in three months.*

Step 2: Break It Down into Actionable Steps

Set three measurable milestones to track progress.

Example:

- Run 1 mile without stopping by Week 2.
- Increase to 3 miles by Month 2.
- Complete a full 5K in Month 3.

Step 3: Identify Obstacles & Solutions

Consider what might go wrong and plan ways to stay on track.

Examples:

- *Obstacle:* Lack of motivation → *Solution:* Find an accountability partner.
- *Obstacle:* Bad weather → *Solution:* Have an indoor workout alternative.

Step 4: Set a Contingency Plan

Decide how you'll adjust if setbacks occur.

Examples:

- If I miss a week of training, I'll modify my schedule rather than quit.
- If progress is slow, I'll extend my timeline instead of getting discouraged.

Step 5: Visualize & Commit

Picture yourself succeeding—feel the emotions, rewards, and sense of accomplishment.

Write a commitment statement:

"I commit to running a 5K in three months. I will follow my plan, adjust when needed, and keep moving forward, even when challenges arise."

Step 6: Take Immediate Action

Start now with one small step to build momentum.

Example: *Put on running shoes and walk for 10 minutes.*

By following this Stoic Blueprint, you create a structured, resilient approach to success, ensuring progress even in the face of challenges.

5.3 THE IMPORTANCE OF MAKING SUCCESS VISIBLE

Now that you have ensured that you have set clear goals and broken these down into smaller steps, it is also essential to make sure that the goal remains visible, and when you stumble or struggle, you are able to revert to the 'why' of this change. The following exercises will support you when you experience bumps along the way. Try to complete all of them to ensure you have this safety net whenever needed.

Practical Activity 1: The Why

Goals cannot be achieved when there is little clarity over the purpose. It is critical to ask yourself why you want to make this change. The why must be connected to your values and who you are as a person. The why should not be connected to other uncontrollable factors, such as external validation from others. Finding the why may take time or may immediately rise to the surface for you. Deploy Stoic meditation or quiet reflection to identify your why. Once you have it, ensure you have written or recorded this somewhere salient to you. It could be on the kitchen fridge, your phone screensaver, or your bathroom mirror. Remembering the why will help you on the tough days and reinforce your purpose.

Practical Activity 2: Positive Visualization

Although we have explored negative visualization in a previous chapter, positive visualization is just as powerful, especially for goal setting and achievement. To complete this activity, find a place that is calm and quiet where you will not be disturbed. Close your eyes and visualize yourself achieving your goal. Fully embrace the result in your mind. Look around you, hear what people are saying and doing, where you are standing, and how you feel. This positive visualization can be used as many times as you would like. It can even be incorporated into a bedtime routine, privately visualizing your success just before you fall asleep. Again, this method helps to reinforce your end goal and the power of achieving it. It can be used when you are faltering or worried you have slipped off course.

Practical Activity 3: Visual Success Board

For some people, merely imagining the end goal or their success is not enough. In this instance, creating a visual board of what your success would look like will really help to support you. Select pictures that would symbolize your success and put them together on one page. Keep this in a salient position in your home, on your phone, or in your bag. This can be referred to at any point in the day when you need a visual reminder about your goals. You could even include your 'why' in the middle of this page as an extra boost.

Practical Activity 4: Tracking Your Success

Success being visible is also clearer when you are able to track your progress over time. Identify a method that will work for you, either a progress tracking app, a device such as a phone, a calendar, or even pen and paper. Record your successes over time and refer to this regularly. The ability to visualize your progress offers another form of reinforcement when you experience a bump in the road on your journey. It also allows you to see how far you have come, providing momentum in moments of challenge.

5.4 BUILDING CONSISTENCY: THE KEY TO LASTING CHANGE

In the Stoic philosophy, consistency is not just a practice but a way of life. It reflects a deep commitment to living by your virtues every day. Whether it's courage, wisdom, or temperance, staying consistent means embodying these qualities in the small actions that make up daily life. This approach aligns with the Stoic belief in steady, incremental progress. Change is not about grand gestures or sudden transformations; it's about the slow, deliberate steps that lead to profound shifts over time. By focusing on consistency, you build a strong foundation that supports lasting change, allowing you to grow in a way that feels natural and sustainable.

Building consistency starts with creating daily routines and habits. This might sound simple, but it requires intentional effort. Establishing consistent daily routines aligned with personal values is essential for building lasting habits. Research indicates that habits account for approximately 40% of our daily behaviors, highlighting the significance of intentional habit formation. Start by identifying key areas in your life that align with your values. Whether it's setting aside time for reflection, exercise, or learning, integrate these activities into your daily schedule. Consistency thrives on repetition, so begin with small, manageable actions that you can commit to every day. It has been found that the first two minutes of any habit are the hardest. By ensuring you commit to just two minutes of the habit you want to form, you begin to establish yourself as someone who regularly shows this behavior. For example, if your goal is to establish a regular gym routine, start by dedicating just two minutes to putting on your workout attire. This minimal commitment lowers the barrier to entry and often leads to visiting the gym or completing the entire workout, as initiating the process builds momentum. Over time, consistently performing these small actions can lead to automatic behaviors, effectively embedding the habit into your routine.

As you establish these routines, you'll find that they become second nature, weaving seamlessly into the fabric of your life. To ensure these habits support your long-term goals, set realistic, incremental milestones. These milestones serve as checkpoints, helping you track your progress and adjust your actions as needed. They provide a sense of achievement and direction, reinforcing your commitment to growth.

Despite your best efforts, maintaining consistency can be challenging. Life's unpredictability often throws obstacles in your path, testing your resolve. When setbacks occur, it's crucial to manage them with patience and resilience. Remember that setbacks are not failures but opportunities to learn and adapt. They are not signals that the habit is a failure and should be stopped. Use struggles as a chance to reassess your approach and make necessary adaptations. To maintain momentum, find ways to keep your motivation alive. This might involve revisiting your reasons for pursuing change or seeking inspiration from those who have walked a similar path. Surround yourself with supportive influences, whether through community groups, books, or mentors, to keep your spirits high and your focus sharp.

Motivational dips are another hurdle on the road to consistency. It's natural for enthusiasm to wane over time, but there are strategies to reignite your passion. Sometimes, people view this as an excuse to avoid their commitments to a habit. Yet you are in control of what you think, your emotional responses, and your actions. Therefore, the ability to start and maintain a habit is well within your control. Reconnect with the original purpose behind your goals. What inspired you to start this journey? Visual reminders, such as vision boards or written affirmations, can help you stay connected to your purpose. Additionally, celebrate small victories along the way. Acknowledging your progress boosts your confidence and reinforces the value of your efforts. By cultivating a positive mindset, you can navigate periods of low motivation and continue moving forward with determination.

Consider the story of Stephen King, a prolific author whose consistent writing habits have led to remarkable success. King commits to writing 2,000 words daily, even on holidays and birthdays. This unwavering routine has resulted in over 60 published novels and numerous short stories, illustrating how steadfast dedication to daily practice can lead to extraordinary achievements.

Similarly, Serena Williams, one of the most accomplished tennis players, attributes her success to consistent training and discipline. From a young age, Williams maintained a rigorous practice schedule, honing her skills daily. Her commitment to consistency has earned her multiple Grand Slam titles and a lasting legacy in the sports world. These examples demonstrate that consistent habits, whether in writing or athletic training, are fundamental to achieving significant success.

Establishing successful habits involves creating behaviors that are cued by specific triggers, are easy to perform, and are rewarding. Research shows that habits are automatic responses to environmental cues, strengthened through repetition in consistent contexts. Clear and consistent cues enhance habit formation while simplifying behaviors promote repetition and long-term adherence. Rewards also play a critical role, as engaging in rewarding behaviors triggers dopamine release, reinforcing habit loops. Tracking progress, such as checking off completed tasks, provides immediate positive feedback and strengthens consistency. For instance, establishing a gym routine by placing workout gear by the door serves as a visible cue, simplifies the process, and encourages follow-through. Each workout completed and tracked reinforces motivation, making the habit more sustainable over time. By integrating clear cues, simplifying behaviors, and incorporating rewards, habits become easier to establish and maintain.

Practical Activity: Building Sustainable Habits

Purpose: Create lasting habits by breaking them into small steps, making them easy to follow, and linking them to existing routines.

Step 1: Identify Your Habit

Choose a habit that aligns with your goals (e.g., exercising daily, reading, or drinking more water).

Step 2: Break It Down into Small Steps

Start with small, manageable actions that build consistency.

Example:

- Place workout clothes by the bed.
- Stretch for 2 minutes.
- Do a 10-minute workout.

Step 3: Make It Easy & Rewarding

- Keep cues visible (e.g., shoes by the door for a workout).
- Start small to reduce resistance.
- Track progress with a journal or app.

Step 4: Use Habit Stacking

Attach your habit to an existing routine using:

"After I [current habit], I will [new habit]."

Example:

- After morning coffee, I'll put on workout gear and stretch.

Step 5: Commit & Adjust

- Stay flexible—if something isn't working, tweak the approach instead of quitting.
- Celebrate small wins to reinforce consistency.

By following this method, you create habits that are sustainable, rewarding, and easy to maintain.

Although you may have a range of ideas for the habits that you want to create, ensure that you select one to start with and don't try to implement them all at the same time. Remember that habits are much more successful when they are salient, easy to do, rewarding, and have a prompt as a reminder to complete them. Habit stacking, associating the habit with a pre-existing habit, is a more effective way of prompting a new habit to form.

5.5 EMBRACING MINIMALISM: SIMPLIFYING FOR GREATER FOCUS

Imagine your life as a garden. Over time, weeds of distraction and clutter grow, choking the vibrant plants beneath. Stoicism offers a way to cultivate this garden through minimalism, encouraging you to clear away the unnecessary to let your true priorities flourish. At its heart, Stoic minimalism is about embracing simplicity and sufficiency. It's about recognizing that less can indeed be more and that by focusing on what truly matters, you find clarity and purpose. This philosophy encourages you to evaluate what you hold dear and to let go of what doesn't serve your core values. In doing so, you create space for the essentials that enrich your life.

The benefits of adopting a minimalist approach are profound. By reducing mental clutter, you alleviate stress and make room for greater focus. Imagine the relief of walking into a tidy room where everything is in its place, and you can see the floor. Similarly, when your mind is free from unnecessary distractions, your ability to concentrate on meaningful pursuits increases. You become more present, engaged, and able to invest your energy wisely. Whether it's tackling a work project or spending quality time with loved ones, minimalism allows you to approach each task with intention and attention, enhancing your overall well-being.

To bring minimalism into your life, begin by decluttering both your physical and digital spaces. Look around your home and identify items that no longer bring you joy or serve a purpose. Donate or recycle what you can, and then organize the rest. In the digital realm, unsubscribe from emails that clutter your inbox and delete apps that distract you. Simplifying your environment creates a ripple effect, making it easier to clear your mind as well. Once you've tackled your surroundings, prioritize your essential goals and activities. Determine what aligns with your values and let go of commitments that drain your time and energy. This intentional focus on what truly matters helps you live a life of purpose and fulfillment.

Real-life examples of minimalism showcase its transformative power. Consider the co-founder of Apple Inc., Steve Jobs, who was renowned for his minimalist approach, both in his personal life, professional life, and in product design. He believed in "simplifying complexity," which was evident in the clean lines and intuitive interfaces of Apple products. Even Jobs's personal wardrobe often consisted of simple black turtlenecks and jeans, reflecting his commitment to minimalism.

As you embrace minimalism, notice how it shifts your perspective. You begin to see the value in simplicity, recognizing that life is not about accumulating more but about appreciating what you have. This shift fosters a sense of gratitude and contentment, helping you find joy in the present moment. By aligning your actions with your true priorities, you create a life that is not only simpler but richer in meaning. As you continue to explore the Stoic principles, remember that minimalism is not an endpoint but a way of living that supports your growth and well-being.

Practical Activity: Embracing Minimalism for Clarity and Focus

Purpose: Simplify your physical, digital, and social life to reduce distractions and create space for focus and fulfillment.

Step 1: Declutter Your Physical Space

A tidy environment promotes mental clarity. Work through these steps:

- Find a place for items cluttering surfaces.
- Remove unnecessary objects from tables and countertops.
- Empty and reassess drawers—keep only what you use.
- Go through cupboards—donate or discard unused items.

Step 2: Simplify Your Digital Life

A cluttered digital space can be overwhelming. Take time to streamline:

- Unsubscribe from unnecessary emails.
- Organize your inbox with folders.
- Delete unused apps and adjust notification settings.
- Cancel subscriptions you no longer use.

Step 3: Reassess Social Commitments

Evaluate how you invest your time and energy:

- Reduce time on social media platforms that no longer serve you.
- Reflect on friendships—are any one-sided or emotionally draining?
- Avoid social obligations made out of guilt rather than genuine interest.

Step 4: Take Action

Choose three immediate steps to simplify your life, such as:

- Clearing one space (desk, closet, kitchen).
- Unsubscribing from five unnecessary emails.
- Setting boundaries around a draining social commitment.

By consistently simplifying, you create mental clarity, reduce stress, and make room for what truly matters.

5.6 LIFELONG LEARNING: STOICISM AS A CONTINUOUS PATH

Imagine life as a vast library, each book representing experiences, knowledge, and wisdom waiting to be discovered. Stoicism encourages you to wander through this library with curiosity and openness, embracing lifelong learning as a dynamic journey. The Stoics believed in the relentless pursuit of wisdom, viewing life as a continual opportunity for growth, not just in intellect but in character. This perspective transforms learning into a living process, where each day holds the potential to teach you something new. It's about remaining open to possibilities and seeking knowledge not only from books but also from interactions, challenges, and even failures. This book is, therefore, not the end but the beginning of your journey. The exercises within the book can be embraced, practiced, and applied across your life, but the ideas should have sparked a further interest in exploring relevant topics at a deeper level. Hopefully, they sparked your interest in exploring your inner wants, needs, and desires at a deeper level.

To cultivate this growth mindset, engage with a diverse range of perspectives and experiences. Start by surrounding yourself with people who challenge your thinking and broaden your horizons. Join discussions, attend workshops, or simply engage in conversations that push you beyond your comfort zone. This exposure to different viewpoints enriches your understanding and helps dismantle biases, fostering a more inclusive worldview. Set ongoing learning goals that stretch your capabilities. Whether it's picking up a new language, studying a different culture, or exploring a new scientific concept, these goals keep your mind active and engaged. Each challenge you set for yourself becomes a stepping stone toward wisdom, encouraging you to evolve and adapt constantly.

Incorporating learning into daily life doesn't require monumental changes. Allocate a few minutes each day for reading and reflection, allowing yourself to digest new information. Choose books and articles that inspire and provoke thought, making them companions in your quest for understanding. Reflect on what you've learned, considering how it applies to your life, your values, and Stoic principles. Alternatively, beyond traditional learning, explore new skills and hobbies that align with your interests. Whether it's painting, coding, or gardening, these activities stimulate your creativity and offer practical applications of your learning. Embrace them with curiosity, letting each new endeavor teach you about the world and yourself.

Throughout history, many have exemplified the Stoic commitment to lifelong learning. Philosophers and scholars like Seneca and Marcus Aurelius continuously sought knowledge, not for its own sake, but to enhance their understanding of life and virtue. Their writings reveal a deep engagement with both philosophical texts and the practical challenges of their time.

An example of lifelong learning in modern times is Richard Branson, the founder of the Virgin Group. Branson started with a small record store and transformed his business empire into a global conglomerate spanning industries from music to airlines. Throughout his career, Branson has consistently embraced new challenges and areas of learning, from space travel with Virgin Galactic to sustainable business practices. His curiosity, openness to new ideas, and continuous learning have allowed him to adapt and thrive in diverse fields, embodying the Stoic principle of lifelong learning and personal growth. Another modern example is Oprah Winfrey, who started with a career in television but has continually expanded her knowledge and influence into areas such as writing, leadership, and philanthropy. Her openness to new ideas and continuous personal growth have made her a role model for lifelong learning and reinvention.

These examples from both history and modern times illustrate that learning is not just an academic pursuit; it is a way of life. Whether it is mastering new technologies, expanding one's influence, or overcoming personal challenges, lifelong learning enriches the individual and benefits society as a whole.

As you embrace this path, remember that Stoicism encourages you to find joy in the process of learning, not just the outcomes. Each lesson, whether from success or failure, adds to the tapestry of your life, weaving a narrative of growth and understanding. This perspective shifts your focus from mere accumulation of knowledge to the cultivation of wisdom, where learning becomes a source of fulfillment and purpose. By integrating these principles into your life, you not only expand your intellectual horizons but also deepen your connection with the world and others.

Practical Activity: Continual Growth

Take a moment to reflect on a skill, subject, or discipline you've been curious about but haven't pursued yet—perhaps because it seemed too time-consuming or complex. Write down a list of areas you're interested in exploring further. Then, think about ways you can start learning more—whether through a local workshop, an online course, a class, or even reading a book.

Make a commitment to set aside dedicated time within the next week to begin this journey of growth. Even if it's just a tiny investment of time, this commitment can significantly expand your current understanding. Often, what starts as a simple curiosity can evolve into a fulfilling hobby and lead to new connections with others who share similar passions.

Taking time each week to grow and learn helps break the monotony of daily routines, feeding your soul in a way that repetitive tasks cannot. It opens up opportunities for personal development, new experiences, and greater fulfillment. Start today—take that first step toward building a new skill or broadening your horizons. The journey of growth begins with a single decision to learn more!

As we move to the next chapter, to learn about applying Stoic principles to our relationships, carry with you the importance of establishing self-discipline and focus. Use the quote below for a final reflection.

> *"No man is free who is not master of himself."*
>
> — EPICTETUS, DISCOURSES

6
IMPROVING AND GROWING INTERPERSONAL RELATIONSHIPS

"Act by everyone, in the same manner as if you supposed yourself to be him, and him to be you."

— HIEROCLES, ELEMENTS OF ETHICS

Picture yourself at a bustling café, conversations buzzing around you. Across from a friend, each exchanged word is a delicate dance. This seemingly ordinary moment captures the essence of deep connection—built on empathy, understanding, and genuine care. In a fast-paced world filled with distractions, authentic interactions can feel rare. Stoicism offers a refreshing perspective, guiding us to cultivate relationships that are both resilient and fulfilling.

Stark findings bring to light the importance of cultivating healthy, meaningful relationships, with many of us spending less time with friends than previously. The Harvard Study of Adult Development, one of the longest-running studies on human well-being, emphasizes that strong, committed relationships are vital for longevity and mental acuity. Maintaining these bonds doesn't require grand gestures; consistent, small actions like sending a text, note, or card can significantly strengthen connections. Research indicates that frequent communication is essential in sustaining friendships, even when in-person meetings are infrequent.

6.1 PRACTICING EMPATHY: SEEING THROUGH THE EYES OF OTHERS

In the realm of Stoicism, empathy is not just an emotional response but a rational understanding of others' experiences. This perspective allows you to engage with others without being swept away by their emotions, maintaining your own emotional balance. Stoic empathy involves recognizing the interconnectedness of all individuals, as Marcus Aurelius, a prominent Stoic philosopher, often emphasized. He believed that viewing others with compassion and understanding was essential for fostering unity and a sense of belonging. In essence, empathy within Stoicism is about expanding your sense of self to include others, promoting a profound sense of connection and mutual respect.

Practicing Stoic empathy involves techniques that deepen your understanding of others. Active listening—fully engaging without judgment—requires giving full attention, maintaining eye contact, and signaling presence through gestures like nodding. By focusing on the speaker's words and emotions, you validate their experience and create space for open communication. Reflective questioning further strengthens this, encouraging deeper dialogue through thoughtful prompts like, *"How did that make you feel?"* or *"What led you to that conclusion?"*

The benefits of empathy are profound. It enhances communication by reducing misunderstandings rooted in assumptions. Approaching interactions with empathy fosters trust and openness, strengthening relationships and creating deeper connections. This mutual understanding enriches both personal and professional relationships, bridging gaps and improving teamwork.

Historical examples provide insight into the power of Stoic empathy. During his reign as Roman Emperor, Marcus Aurelius practiced empathy by listening carefully to his advisors and subjects, striving to understand their needs and concerns. His ability to empathize with others allowed him to lead with compassion and wisdom, ensuring that his decisions aligned with the greater good. In modern times, consider Sarina Wiegman, the head coach of the England women's football team, who showcases empathetic leadership by maintaining open and honest communication with her players. Her direct yet understanding approach has been pivotal in building resilient and emotionally intelligent teams, leading to significant successes on the field. Wiegman's emphasis on empathy fosters strong relationships and a cohesive team environment. Such examples illustrate how Stoic empathy, when applied thoughtfully, can transform relationships and create a more harmonious and understanding world.

Reflection Activity: Practicing Empathy in Everyday Interactions

Purpose: Strengthen relationships by improving active listening and empathy in conversations.

Step 1: Reflect on a Past Interaction

Think of a conversation where more empathy could have improved the outcome. Ask yourself:

- What was the situation?
- How did you respond?
- How might empathy or active listening have changed the dynamic?
- Write down key insights from this experience.

Step 2: Develop Empathy Strategies

Consider ways to actively practice empathy:

- **Active Listening:** Give full attention, make eye contact, and avoid interrupting.
- **Reflective Questioning:** Ask open-ended questions to encourage discussion.
- **Emotional Validation:** Acknowledge feelings before offering solutions.
- **Paraphrasing for Clarity:** Repeat key points to confirm understanding (e.g., "It sounds like you're feeling...").
- **Nonverbal Cues:** Use open body language and a calm tone to show engagement.

Step 3: Use Supportive Conversation Prompts

Practice using phrases like:

- *"It sounds like this has been really challenging. Can you tell me more?"*
- *"I hear that you're feeling [emotion]. What do you think would help most?"*
- *"That must have been difficult—how are you holding up?"*
- *"I appreciate you sharing this. How can I support you?"*

Step 4: Apply Empathy in an Upcoming Conversation

- Who will you be speaking with?
- What challenges might arise?
- How can you use active listening strategies to improve the conversation?

Take a moment beforehand to review key prompts and remind yourself to listen before responding.

Step 5: Reflect on the Conversation

Afterward, ask yourself:

- What went well?
- Did you listen more attentively or ask better questions?
- How did the other person respond?
- What can you improve next time?

By consistently practicing and refining your approach, you build stronger, more meaningful connections.

6.2 FOSTERING RELATIONSHIPS: THE IMPORTANCE OF APPRECIATION

As we have discovered in previous chapters, gratitude for the small things in life is critical to Stoic philosophy. Gratitude is crucial for maintaining and strengthening relationships. Research supports the critical role of communication in maintaining healthy relationships and highlights the importance of balancing negative interactions with positive ones. Effective communication is foundational to relationship satisfaction. Studies have shown that negative communication patterns, such as criticism, contempt, defensiveness, and stonewalling, are strong predictors of relationship dissatisfaction and dissolution. These behaviors can create a cycle of negativity, leading to emotional disengagement and, ultimately, the breakdown of the relationship.

Renowned psychologist Dr. John Gottman introduced the concept of the "magic ratio," which posits that stable and happy relationships exhibit a ratio of five positive interactions for every negative one during conflicts. This balance acts as a buffer, allowing couples to navigate disagreements more effectively and maintain an emotional connection. Gottman's research involved observing couples' interactions and found that this 5:1 ratio was a significant predictor of marital stability. Couples who maintained this ratio were more likely to have enduring and satisfying relationships, whereas those with higher negative-to-positive interaction ratios were at increased risk of divorce.

These findings underscore the importance of fostering positive interactions—such as expressing appreciation, showing empathy, and engaging in affectionate behaviors—to counterbalance negative moments. This is not only in romantic relationships, but in platonic friendships too. By intentionally incorporating positive exchanges, individuals can strengthen their relationships and enhance overall satisfaction.

A method to improve the number of positive interactions is the simple act of vocalizing appreciation. This is essential as many of us often forget that others cannot hear our thoughts. Without telling someone what you appreciate about them, they simply won't know. These vocalizations can be appreciation for simple tasks, such as making you a cup of coffee, giving you a warm hug when you get home from work, or tidying away the dishes. These small appreciations of things that might otherwise go unnoticed or unvoiced are critical for relationship maintenance and allow you to add to those daily deposits in your relationship.

Reflection Activity: Daily Appreciation Commitment

Step 1: Identify an Important Relationship

Take a moment to think of someone in your life whom you sincerely appreciate—a partner, friend, family member, or colleague.

Step 2: Reflect on Your Expressions of Gratitude

- Do you regularly express appreciation for this person?
- How often do you acknowledge the small things they do?
- Are you actively nurturing this relationship with small, thoughtful gestures?

Step 3: Make a Commitment

Decide on one small action you will take to show appreciation regularly. This could be:

- Sending a short message of gratitude each morning.
- Expressing one thing you appreciate about them at the dinner table or before bed.
- Writing a quick thank-you note or voice message.

Step 4: Put It Into Action

Start today—send a message, say a kind word, or make a small gesture to show you value them. Notice how this strengthens your connection over time.

6.3 STOIC RELATIONSHIP FORMATION: THE ROLE OF VALUES

Recent studies have highlighted a significant increase in loneliness among young adults, particularly those aged 18 to 25, as an unintended consequence of the COVID-19 pandemic. While loneliness has often been associated with older populations, data now indicates that younger adults are experiencing higher rates of social isolation. A report from Harvard University revealed that 61% of young adults feel "serious loneliness." Similarly, the U.S. Surgeon General's advisory noted that approximately half of U.S. adults report experiencing loneliness, with some of the highest rates among young adults.

Despite increasing levels of formal education, there remains a lack of emphasis on teaching individuals how to establish and maintain friendships. While forming connections may come more naturally during school or college years, it becomes more challenging as people progress into adulthood. The pandemic has exacerbated this issue, as social distancing measures and lockdowns have limited opportunities for in-person interactions, further hindering the development of meaningful relationships among young adults. Addressing this growing concern requires intentional efforts to foster social connections and equip individuals with the skills necessary to build and sustain friendships throughout their lives.

If you're wondering how to start forming meaningful connections, begin by reflecting on your values, which you identified in Chapter 3 (3.1). Identifying what matters most to you can help guide you when you seek out like-minded individuals. For example, if you highly value fitness and health, consider spending time in environments where others share this passion—gyms, health retreats, healthy cafés, or specialty shops. Being in these spaces naturally provides conversation starters and makes initial interactions easier. As you frequent these places, you can gradually build rapport through regular conversations, eventually leading to deeper connections and potential meet-ups in similar settings.

When interacting with others and suggesting future meet-ups, the key to remember is that the worst outcome is simply a "no". According to the dichotomy of control, you cannot control others' responses, only your own actions. However, if you've been engaging in consistent conversations and crossing paths regularly, chances are they share a similar mindset and may be open to deeper connections. Many people are also searching for meaningful relationships, and by making the first move, you increase the likelihood of forming a genuine bond and supporting the other person with this goal, too.

Similarly, if you value nature, immerse yourself in environments where like-minded individuals gather, such as local parks, nature reserves, or outdoor clubs. Follow the same approach—initiate conversations around shared interests and suggest future meet-ups that align with this value.

Ultimately, remember that you're not just seeking connections for yourself—you may also be offering someone else the opportunity to form a meaningful friendship. In today's loneliness epidemic, many people are longing for deeper relationships. By taking the first step, you're not only enhancing your own social circle but also helping others find the connections they need.

Practical Activity: Finding Connections Through Shared Values

This activity helps you identify places where like-minded individuals gather, making it easier to form meaningful, value-based connections.

Step 1: Identify Your Key Values

Review your personal values and choose one or two that are most important in building relationships (e.g., health, learning, nature).

Step 2: Find Aligned Spaces

Think about where people who share these values gather:

- Fitness & Health: Gyms, yoga studios, running clubs.
- Learning & Growth: Libraries, book clubs, workshops.
- Nature & Outdoors: Parks, hiking groups, nature reserves.

Step 3: Take Action

- Choose one place from your list and visit it.
- Start with small interactions—a greeting, a shared observation, or a friendly question.
- Set a goal: Engage in at least one conversation.

Step 4: Reflect & Adjust

- How did it feel to be in that environment?
- Did you find opportunities to connect?
- Would you go back, or would you prefer to explore a different place?

By taking these small steps, you create opportunities to form meaningful relationships based on shared values.

6.4 BUILDING TRUST AND CONNECTION: STOIC PRINCIPLES IN ACTION

Trust is the bedrock of any strong relationship, whether personal or professional. It's the invisible thread that binds individuals together, allowing them to rely on each other and work toward common goals. In Stoicism, trust is deeply rooted in the virtues of reliability and consistency. These qualities create a stable foundation upon which trust can flourish. When you consistently demonstrate reliability, others learn they can count on you. This consistency breeds confidence and comfort, knowing that your actions align with your words. Moreover, practicing honesty and transparency in interactions reinforces this trust. By clearly communicating your intentions and being open about your limitations, you foster an environment where trust can grow naturally. Transparency, in particular, invites others to do the same, creating a reciprocal dynamic where openness and honesty are valued.

Building trust requires intentional effort and genuine connection. One key strategy is following through on commitments—a simple yet powerful way to demonstrate reliability. Honoring your word shows respect for others' time and values, and even small kept promises strengthen trust. Another essential approach is demonstrating empathy and understanding. Truly listening and acknowledging others' feelings validates their experiences and deepens your bond. This doesn't mean agreeing with everything but being present and attentive, showing that you genuinely care about their emotions and perspectives.

Consider the legacy of Stoic leaders who built trust with their followers through these principles. Marcus Aurelius, for instance, led with integrity and empathy, earning the respect and loyalty of those he governed. His ability to listen and act with sincerity helped him maintain the trust of his subjects even in turbulent times. In modern professional settings, trust remains equally vital. Picture a project manager who consistently meets deadlines and communicates openly with their team. Their reliability and transparency create a supportive environment where team members feel valued and understood. This, in turn, enhances collaboration and productivity, as trust empowers individuals to contribute their best without fear of judgment or failure.

The benefits of building strong trust connections extend beyond the immediate relationship. In a professional context, trust enhances collaboration and teamwork. When team members trust each other, they communicate more freely, share ideas without reservation, and work together toward shared objectives. This synergy leads to innovative solutions and more efficient problem-solving. On a personal level, strong trust connections contribute to greater fulfillment and support networks. Relationships built on trust provide emotional security and a sense of belonging, offering a refuge during challenging times. They enrich your life with deeper connections and shared experiences, fostering a sense of community and well-being.

Trust is not a static quality but a dynamic process that requires ongoing attention and nurturing. By embodying the Stoic virtues of reliability, honesty, and empathy, you can cultivate trust in your relationships, transforming them into sources of strength and inspiration. These principles not only enhance your connections with others but also contribute to your personal growth and fulfillment. As you cultivate trust, you create a ripple effect that extends beyond individual relationships, promoting a culture of openness, understanding, and genuine connection.

Reflection Activity: Trust

Think about a recent promise you made to someone, no matter how small—perhaps agreeing to do the dishes or take out the trash. Did you follow through? How did keeping your word strengthen trust in that relationship? How did the other person respond?

Now, reflect on areas where you sometimes commit to things but struggle to follow through. It's okay to realize you can't always complete everything you promise, but maintaining trust means being honest from the start. Instead of over-committing and letting someone down, practice clear and realistic communication.

We all know the friend who frequently makes plans but rarely follows through. Don't be that person. Consider how you can become more intentional with your commitments and ensure your words align with your actions. How will you build a reputation for reliability and trustworthiness in your future interactions?

6.5 GROWING YOUR POSITIVE IMPACT: CIRCLES OF CONCERN

Understanding the role of community in Stoic practice highlights the profound impact you can have on the world. Hierocles's Circles of Concern illustrate how we can expand empathy beyond ourselves to embrace broader communities. The innermost circle represents the self, followed by family, friends, fellow citizens, and, ultimately, all humanity. This model underscores the importance of recognizing our shared humanity and fostering compassion, even for those distant from us.

At its core, this aligns with the Stoic principle of oikiosis, the natural sense of belonging. Humans have an innate capacity to form connections, beginning with the self and extending outward. Oikiosis reminds us that we are part of a greater whole—bound by shared nature—and encourages us to expand our care beyond our immediate circles. This sense of interconnectedness aligns with the Stoic belief in the importance of virtue and acting in accordance with nature, which includes the acknowledgment that our actions should benefit others and contribute to the common good.

By consciously working to widen these circles, we can build a more inclusive and compassionate worldview. The practice of expanding one's circles of concern involves reflecting on how to care for those outside our immediate family or community. For example, you might start by taking care of their immediate family but then consider how to contribute to the well-being of neighbors, the larger community, or even global issues such as poverty, environmental sustainability, or human rights. Even just one-off offers of support can be impactful. This shift from focusing solely on personal gain to considering the broader impact can help reduce self-centeredness and encourage empathy and compassion for the collective good.

Research supports the positive benefits of expanding our circle of concern and engaging in compassionate behavior beyond our immediate environment. Studies show that acts of kindness and compassion, such as helping strangers or contributing to societal welfare, can have significant benefits for mental and physical health. It also enables you to engage with issues in the present, get out of your own head, and avoid being consumed by your own emotions. Research has found that people who engage in altruistic behaviors experience increased well-being and life satisfaction. Moreover, acts of kindness activate the brain's reward system, releasing feel-good chemicals like dopamine and oxytocin, which in turn enhance emotional well-being and reduce stress.

Additionally, connecting with others and expanding our circles of concern have been shown to improve social cohesion and community resilience. According to research from the American Psychological Association (APA), individuals who engage in social support networks and give back to their communities experience lower rates of depression, greater life satisfaction, and stronger relationships.

Hierocles believed that this expansion of empathy not only strengthens our sense of interconnectedness but also fosters personal growth. As we develop greater compassion for others, we begin to transcend self-interest, aligning our actions with a broader sense of justice and shared humanity. Ultimately, by recognizing and acting upon our shared bonds, we contribute to a more harmonious and resilient society. This broader sense of care and connection can also enhance our sense of purpose as we align our values with the well-being of the greater whole, leading to deeper fulfillment and a lasting positive impact.

Practical Activity: Expanding Your Circles of Concern

Explore how to apply the Stoic principle of *oikiosis* by broadening your empathy and engagement beyond yourself.

Step 1: Start with Yourself

Reflect on how you are caring for your physical, emotional, and mental well-being. What can you do to support yourself so you can engage with others from a place of strength?

Step 2: Expand to Family & Friends

Consider how you contribute to the well-being of your closest relationships. How can you deepen connections, show kindness, or offer more support?

Step 3: Broaden to Your Community

Think about ways to engage with those beyond your immediate circle—neighbors, coworkers, or community members. Can you extend small acts of kindness, get more involved, or offer help where needed?

Step 4: Consider Society at Large

Reflect on global concerns such as poverty, sustainability, or inequality. What small steps can you take to contribute meaningfully—

through lifestyle changes, volunteering, or supporting causes that align with your values?

Step 5: Take Action & Reflect

- Choose one action to take in each area this week.
- Reflect on how expanding your circles of concern makes you feel more connected and engaged.

By practicing this, you cultivate a more compassionate, interconnected worldview—enriching both your life and the lives of those around you.

6.6 STOIC COMMUNICATION: SPEAKING WITH CLARITY AND PURPOSE

In our daily lives, relationships are not only confined to friends and family but also extend to our everyday interactions and work. Sometimes, it can be tricky to navigate these relationships, too. The remainder of the chapter will inform your approach to navigating relationships with clarity and would benefit from being applied to a whole range of situations or contexts.

Imagine sitting across from a colleague in a meeting. The room is filled with tension as you navigate the complexities of a challenging discussion. At this moment, the principles of Stoic communication come into play, emphasizing the power of clarity and purpose in speech. Stoicism teaches that honest and integrity-driven dialogue not only reflects your values but also fosters genuine connections. The emphasis here is on speaking with intention, ensuring that your words align with your beliefs and contribute meaningfully to the conversation. This approach means you choose your words carefully, are aware of their impact, and are committed to truthfulness. When you communicate with integrity, you build trust, a cornerstone of any lasting relationship.

Sometimes, we avoid having conversations that we perceive as difficult. We may instead put them off or send our thoughts in written form. Not only does this delay the conversation that needs to be had, but it can also lead to further miscommunication and misconceptions arising from the written words. By engaging with others face-to-face, we allow ourselves and them to speak honestly but also avoid ambiguities or misinterpretations. We can make clear our intentions and clarify where needed.

To enhance the clarity and purpose of your conversations, consider structuring your thoughts before speaking. This preparation allows you to articulate your ideas coherently, reducing misunderstandings. Before a conversation, take a moment to organize your thoughts, identifying the key points you wish to convey. This mental rehearsal ensures that your message is clear and direct. Additionally, using concise language helps convey your message effectively without unnecessary embellishments. Being succinct not only respects the listener's time but also enhances the strength of your message. By focusing on clarity, you invite others to engage with your ideas openly, fostering an environment where communication flows freely and purposefully.

Handling difficult conversations with Stoic calm is challenging but rewarding. Start with active listening and thoughtful responses. When emotions run high, Stoicism urges you to pause and reflect before reacting (see Chapter 2, 2.1). This moment of restraint helps you consider the other person's perspective and choose your words wisely.

Managing emotional reactions is crucial. As tensions rise, stay composed and focus on the issue rather than personal attacks. If the conversation becomes too heated, you have the right to state that you'd like to pause and revisit it later when both parties are calmer. This often gives the other person time to process your message before re-engaging.

Throughout, focus on what you can control—your thoughts, emotions, and actions. If the other person reacts emotionally, that is beyond your control. Your power lies in maintaining your own composure and responding with clarity and intention.

The benefits of Stoic communication extend far beyond individual interaction, shaping the very fabric of your relationships. Clear communication fosters improved mutual understanding, as both parties feel heard and valued. This understanding paves the way for deeper trust as you demonstrate reliability in your words and actions. With trust comes reduced conflict, as misunderstandings are minimized and collaboration is enhanced. When you communicate with clarity and purpose, you create a foundation for relationships that are resilient and harmonious, capable of weathering life's inevitable challenges.

Practical Activity: Difficult Conversation Preparation

Think about an upcoming difficult conversation you need to have—whether with a colleague, friend, or family member. Use the steps below to prepare for a transparent, constructive, and emotionally balanced discussion.

Step 1: Clarify Your Key Messages

- Write down the **main points** you need to communicate. Keep them short and focused.
- **Practice saying them aloud.** Is your message clear and concise? Could it be refined?
- If needed, jot down **a few notes** to use as a reference during the conversation.

Step 2: Anticipate and Manage Emotions

- What emotions might **you** experience?
- How might the **other person** react?

- Plan how you will **stay calm and focused** by remembering that emotions are signals, not commands. You can evaluate them later instead of reacting impulsively.

Step 3: Keep the Conversation on Track

- If tensions rise or the discussion derails, how will you **pause or redirect** the conversation?
- Rehearse a **neutral, non-confrontational phrase** to use if emotions escalate. For example:
  - *"I want to continue this conversation, but I think we both need a moment to process."*
  - *"Let's take a break and revisit this when we're both in a better place to talk."*

By preparing your key points, staying mindful of emotions, and planning for potential challenges, you can approach difficult conversations with confidence, clarity, and a greater chance of a positive outcome.

6.7 HANDLING CRITICISM AND CONFLICT WITH STOIC GRACE

Criticism can feel like a sting, but through the lens of Stoicism, it transforms into an opportunity for growth. The Stoics encourage us to detach personal judgment from criticism, perceiving it not as a personal attack but as valuable feedback. This perspective is liberating. It allows you to step back and view criticism objectively, recognizing its potential to highlight areas for improvement. By reframing criticism as a chance to refine your skills and understanding, you can embrace it with curiosity rather than defensiveness. This approach not only enhances personal growth but also fosters a mindset that is open to change and learning. It shifts the focus from self-preservation to self-improvement, encouraging you to welcome diverse perspectives and insights.

Responding to criticism with composure and grace involves a few key strategies. First, it's crucial to pause before reacting (see Chapter 2, 2.1). This brief moment of reflection allows you to assess the validity of the criticism, distinguishing constructive feedback from baseless negativity. By taking this pause, you gain clarity and prevent knee-jerk reactions that might escalate the situation. Remember the dichotomy of control in this instance, too. You cannot control what another person thinks about you. It is not possible. Trying to control what someone thinks about you is futile. Accept it for what it is: another person's thoughts and one person's perspective, but remember that they do not have to influence you emotionally. As a reminder of the dichotomy of control and not allowing others to have power over you, revisit Chapter 1 (1.2).

Another technique is to express gratitude for constructive feedback. Thanking someone for their critique, even if it stings, acknowledges the courage it takes to offer honest opinions. It also reinforces a culture of open communication, where feedback is seen as a tool for mutual growth. This gratitude not only diffuses tension but also invites further dialogue, creating a space for understanding and collaboration. It may lead you to a blind spot that you had not considered before and an opportunity for growth in this area.

Managing conflict through Stoic practices means focusing on shared goals and values rather than differences. While perspectives may clash, common ground often exists. Recognizing this shifts the focus from opposition to collaboration. Patience and understanding are key Stoic strategies. Actively listening—especially when views differ—creates a space where all parties feel heard and respected, leading to fair resolutions. This is especially vital in conflicts with those close to us, as their criticism often comes from concern for our well-being. By approaching conflict with understanding, you turn tension into an opportunity for connection and growth.

Handling criticism and conflict well goes beyond personal growth: it strengthens relationships by fostering resilience and emotional maturity. Responding to criticism with grace models emotional intelligence, inspiring others to do the same. This maturity earns respect, as people admire your ability to stay composed under pressure. Gracefully managing conflict also builds trust. When people feel safe expressing themselves, knowing they'll be met with understanding, relationships deepen. Differences become opportunities for connection rather than division.

History offers powerful examples, such as Marcus Aurelius, who, as emperor, faced relentless criticism yet saw challenges as chances to grow. His *Meditations* reveal a commitment to self-improvement despite external pressures. In modern settings, a strong leader who handles workplace conflicts with clarity and shared goals fosters teamwork and creativity. These examples show how Stoic principles turn criticism and conflict into catalysts for deeper growth and connection.

Reflection Activity: Receiving Criticism

Think about a recent experience where you faced criticism or conflict. How did you react? What emotions surfaced? Did you approach the feedback with curiosity, seeing it as an opportunity to understand another perspective? Or did emotions take over, making it difficult to stay objective?

Consider how Stoic principles could have influenced the outcome. Did you remind yourself that while you cannot control others' opinions, you can control your response? How might pausing before reacting or focusing on shared goals have improved the conversation? Reflect on how shifting your mindset could help you embrace criticism as a tool for growth rather than a personal attack.

Receiving Criticism Phrases

Use the phrases below to navigate criticism with composure and openness:

- *"I appreciate your perspective—can you help me understand more?"*
- *"That's an interesting point. Let me take some time to reflect on it."*
- *"I hadn't considered that before. Can you share an example?"*
- *"Thank you for the feedback. I'll think about how I can apply it."*
- *"I understand your concern. Let's find a way to work through this together."*

By practicing these responses, you reinforce self-control, humility, and growth, making future criticism feel less like a challenge and more like an opportunity to refine your thinking and actions.

6.8 NAVIGATING DIFFICULT RELATIONSHIPS: PATIENCE AND DETACHMENT

Relationships can be messy, filled with misunderstandings and emotional highs and lows. Navigating the difficult ones takes more than just endurance—it requires Stoic patience and detachment. Patience isn't just waiting without complaint; it's the quiet strength to endure discomfort, to hold steady when emotions run high, and to wait for clarity without frustration. Detachment doesn't mean indifference—it's the ability to stay grounded amidst others' emotional storms, engaging with presence rather than reacting impulsively. Together, patience and detachment form a powerful duo, helping you face difficult interactions with grace, resilience, and a clear mind.

Managing complex relationships is an art that requires setting boundaries while remaining open to dialogue. Boundaries are essential for protecting your emotional well-being, ensuring that interactions do not drain your energy or compromise your values. These boundaries should be clear yet flexible enough to allow meaningful conversations. These boundaries are essential to set for yourself with all relationships and should be followed and reviewed regularly.

Detaching from difficult relationships starts with embracing the dichotomy of control—you cannot control what others think, feel, or do. Accepting this frees you from the burden of keeping others happy or prioritizing their needs over your own. If someone is annoyed, frustrated, or in a negative mood, it is not a reflection of you. Their emotions are their responsibility to process and manage. While offering support through active listening and empathy is valuable, be mindful of those who consistently offload their emotions onto you or expect you to "fix" their problems. Their emotional state is not your responsibility, and recognizing this is crucial for protecting your well-being.

This boundary is not just about how others treat you—it also requires self-awareness. Do you expect others to make you happy or improve your mood? Just as you cannot control another person's emotions, they cannot control yours. True detachment means recognizing when someone is experiencing intense emotions and understanding that you are not responsible for solving them. It allows you to remain grounded, preventing their emotional turbulence from overwhelming you.

Without detachment, you risk becoming emotionally flooded yourself, reducing your ability to think clearly or offer rational advice. This happens because stress hormones trigger your body's stress response cycle, as explored in Chapter 2 (2.1). Detachment is not indifference—it is a necessary skill for maintaining balance in relationships where others may expect you to absorb their emotional burdens. By setting clear boundaries, you protect your emotional well-being and ensure that your support for others remains thoughtful rather than draining.

Stories of individuals who have successfully navigated challenging relationships using Stoic principles offer valuable insights. Consider the historical figure of Seneca, who maintained harmony despite the political turbulence around him. His ability to exercise patience and detachment allowed him to navigate complex relationships in the Roman court, demonstrating the power of these virtues. In modern times, think of a parent dealing with a rebellious teenager. By practicing patience and setting clear boundaries, this parent can maintain a relationship based on mutual respect and understanding. Over time, the child might begin to see their parent not as an adversary but as a supportive ally. These examples highlight how patience and detachment foster resilience and understanding, transforming difficult relationships into opportunities for growth.

Stoic patience and detachment benefit more than just your relationships—they enhance your well-being. By reducing stress and emotional strain, you free up mental energy for meaningful interactions. Staying calm amid others' struggles helps you focus on what matters without feeling overwhelmed. This steadiness strengthens your connections, creating a buffer against life's emotional ups and downs. With this mindset, challenges become opportunities to build deeper, more resilient relationships.

Practical Activity: Practicing Detachment in Difficult Relationships

Purpose: Strengthen emotional resilience by maintaining clarity and balance in challenging interactions.

Step 1: Reflect on a Recent Emotional Encounter

Think of a situation where someone's emotions overwhelmed you.

- What happened?
- How did they feel? How did you feel?
- Were you able to support them without becoming emotionally drained?

Step 2: Apply Stoic Detachment

Revisit the situation through a Stoic lens:

- When could you have reminded yourself of what you can and cannot control?
- How could you have stayed calm and detached?
- What strategies could you have used to listen without absorbing their emotions?
- How could you have shown empathy while maintaining emotional boundaries?

Step 3: Plan for Future Encounters

Identify 1–2 strategies to use in similar situations:

- **Pause before reacting.**
- **Use a mental reminder:** *"I can control my response, not their emotions."*
- **Set boundaries:** Avoid taking on their emotional burden.

Step 4: Evaluate Your Boundaries

- Are your boundaries clear to both you and the other person?
- Have they been communicated effectively?
- Do they need to be adjusted based on past interactions?

By practicing detachment, you build resilience and navigate difficult relationships with greater balance and self-awareness.

As we conclude this chapter, consider how applying Stoic principles to your relationships can transform them into sources of strength and growth. By practicing patience, managing emotions, and fostering meaningful connections, you enrich all interactions. Next, we'll explore how Stoicism helps you navigate modern challenges with clarity and resilience. However, first, revisit the importance of kindness by reflecting on the following quote.

> *"Kindness is invincible, but only when it's sincere, with no hypocrisy or faking. Because what can even the most aggressive person do if you keep treating him with kindness and gently set him straight?"*
>
> — MARCUS AURELIUS, MEDITATIONS

7
OVERCOMING MODERN LIFE'S CHALLENGES

"If you are pained by an external thing, it is not the thing that disturbs you, but your judgment about it. And it is in your power to wipe out this judgment now."

— MARCUS AURELIUS, MEDITATIONS

Picture this: You're at your desk, screen glowing, emails piling up, and a looming deadline weighing on you. In today's fast-paced work environment, stress feels constant —high expectations, tight deadlines, and interpersonal conflicts only add to the pressure. Miscommunication breeds tension, further draining your well-being. Here, Stoicism offers a beacon of hope, helping you navigate challenges with resilience and clarity.

7.1 NAVIGATING DIFFICULT SITUATIONS: DETACHMENT FROM OUTCOMES

The essence of Stoic thought lies in controlling your response to external events, a principle that can transform how you handle stress at work. We have just looked at practicing detachment from another person's emotions to ensure that we do not get overwhelmed by their feelings in Chapter 6 (6.7). Another form of detachment, referred to as detachment from outcomes, is critical for helping you to learn to focus on the process rather than the result. This shift in perspective reduces the anxiety tied to achieving specific results, allowing you to concentrate on what you can control—your actions, emotional reactions, and thoughts. When faced with tense moments, such as a heated meeting or a tight deadline, employing deep breathing and mindfulness techniques can help you maintain composure. This mindfulness fosters a rational response, preventing impulsive reactions that often exacerbate stress.

Enhancing focus and productivity with Stoic practices involves setting clear priorities aligned with your values. Start by identifying what truly matters and eliminating distractions that do not serve your goals. Discipline your focus by creating a structured environment that minimizes interruptions. This could mean setting specific times to check emails or using tools to block distracting websites. Such discipline enables you to engage fully with your tasks, increasing efficiency and satisfaction.

Despite the misconception that multitasking is efficient, research has consistently shown that it negatively impacts task completion and focus. Individuals who frequently engage in multitasking perform worse on tasks requiring sustained attention and cognitive control. By concentrating on one task at a time, you can achieve a state of flow where productivity and creativity flourish, making work not only bearable but fulfilling.

Sometimes, we ponder too much about the destination or the bigger picture that we are trying to achieve. Detaching from this when trying to meet deadlines allows you to focus on achieving the smaller goals along the way. Preoccupation with the outcome can quickly turn to worrying and procrastination. By detaching from the outcome and accepting that you can only control your current thoughts, emotional reactions, and actions, you can refocus on the task at hand.

Real-world applications of these Stoic strategies abound, offering inspiration for those seeking to thrive professionally. Consider Jack Dorsey, co-founder of Twitter and Square, who has spoken about the importance of disciplined focus in his work without becoming preoccupied with the outcomes. Faced with the demands of running two major companies simultaneously, Dorsey structured his days with intentional focus, assigning different tasks to specific days and minimizing distractions—an approach reminiscent of Stoic time management. Instead of being consumed by anxiety over the sheer volume of responsibilities or potential future eventualities, he concentrated on the present moment, prioritizing what he could control. This disciplined approach allowed him to operate efficiently and make strategic decisions without being overwhelmed. His experience demonstrates how Stoicism can serve as a practical tool for managing the complexities of modern work life.

Practical Activity: Prioritizing with Purpose

Step 1: Identify Your Key Priorities

- List three tasks from your current workload that align with your core values and long-term goals.
- Consider why these tasks matter to you and how they contribute to your personal or professional growth.

Step 2: Minimize Distractions

- Identify one major distraction that disrupts your focus (e.g., phone notifications, multitasking, or unnecessary meetings).
- Write down one specific action you will take today to reduce this distraction.

Step 3: Detach from long-term outcomes

- Remind yourself of the importance of avoiding preoccupation with potential scenarios in the future.
- Reaffirm your understanding of relying on what is immediately within your control and take steps within the present moment to build towards a larger goal.

Step 4: Apply a Stoic Principle

- Choose one Stoic technique to help you work with greater focus and intention. Some options include:
  - *Dichotomy of Control* – Focus only on what is within your power.
  - *Amor Fati* – Accept challenges as opportunities to grow.
- Write down how you will apply this technique to your workday.

By aligning tasks with values, eliminating distractions, and applying Stoic wisdom, you create a more focused, resilient, and fulfilling work environment.

7.2 FINANCIAL STRESS: STOIC PERSPECTIVES ON WEALTH AND SECURITY

In a world driven by consumerism, where financial success often equates to personal worth, Stoicism offers a refreshing perspective on wealth and material possessions. This ancient philosophy regards wealth as indifferent—it's neither inherently good nor bad. Instead, Stoicism acknowledges financial security as a tool that is useful for achieving a life of virtue and tranquility. The Stoics believed in sufficiency over excess, advocating for a life where needs are met and desires are tempered. This approach encourages us to distinguish between wants, which are often insatiable, and needs, which are finite and attainable. By focusing on sufficiency, you can cultivate a sense of contentment, freeing yourself from the relentless pursuit of more.

Managing financial stress through Stoic principles involves a shift in mindset. It starts with practicing gratitude for what you already have (see Chapter 1, 1.5). By appreciating your current resources, you redirect focus from scarcity to abundance, reducing anxiety about financial inadequacy. Embracing frugality and mindful spending also plays a crucial role. It's not about depriving yourself but about making intentional choices that align with your values. When you spend money, consider whether the purchase adds genuine value or merely satisfies a fleeting desire. This mindfulness not only curtails unnecessary expenses but also nurtures a more profound sense of fulfillment as your financial decisions reflect your core values.

Picture a man in a sleek, expensive suit sitting alone in his corner office at 10 p.m. He's still working, chasing the next dollar, the next promotion, the luxury car, and the bigger house. From the outside, he appears powerful and successful by society's standards. But what no one asks is—how does he feel? Is he fulfilled? Is he happy?

Society often defines success by wealth, status, and possessions because they're easy to measure. But fulfillment, the true marker of a meaningful life, is harder to quantify. Research shows that chasing external validation leads to a cycle of never feeling satisfied. The key question is: What is enough for me? Without a personal definition of success, you risk endlessly pursuing more without contentment.

Everything has a cost. We celebrate billion-dollar companies but rarely acknowledge the sacrifices behind them—strained relationships, missed experiences, and declining well-being. Instead of chasing the next financial milestone, Stoicism urges us to ask: Do I have enough? The answer isn't in a paycheck but in living within your means while staying true to your values and well-being.

Consider two individuals with different incomes. Person A earns $4,100 per month but, after covering expenses for housing, transportation, food, and clothing, is left with only $100 in savings. In contrast, Person B earns significantly less at $1,600 per month but, after similar expenses, retains $500. Despite earning more, Person A is in a weaker financial position, while Person B has the flexibility to save or invest. Over time, the power of compounding allows Person B's investments to grow at a much faster rate than Person A's. This illustrates the fundamental principle of living within our means and prioritizing saving or investing. Making this simple shift can be the key to achieving financial stability and a debt-free lifestyle. To explore this further, use the activity below to audit your spending.

Building financial resilience with Stoic practices requires a proactive approach. If there are explicit things that you are aiming for, setting realistic financial goals that prioritize stability and growth is critical for success. These goals should reflect your values, ensuring they support both your current needs and future aspirations. Investing in personal growth and well-being is equally important. Allocate resources towards education, skills development, and health, as these investments yield long-term benefits. This approach not only fortifies your financial foundation but also enhances your overall quality of life as you cultivate skills and habits that contribute to lasting prosperity. If you want to explore goal-setting in more detail, revisit Chapter 5 (5.2). By aligning your financial strategies with Stoic values, you create a sustainable framework for financial health, one that withstands the uncertainties of life.

Financial well-being is not solely about accumulating wealth but also about aligning financial practices with personal values. By adopting Stoic perspectives on wealth and security, you can transform financial stress into an opportunity for growth and contentment. By stopping to assess whether you have enough and defining your own version of success, you can live in alignment with your values. It's about recognizing that true prosperity extends beyond monetary wealth, encompassing a life of intention, wisdom, and peace of mind. As you navigate your financial journey, remember that the principles of Stoicism offer a steady guide, helping you cultivate a life where financial security supports you and enriches your experiences.

Practical Activity: Living Within Your Means Audit

Purpose: Gain financial awareness by tracking, categorizing, and evaluating your spending habits to align them with your values and needs.

Step 1: Track Your Spending

- Identify your monthly income.
- Record your expenses for a week, then multiply by four to estimate monthly spending.
- Include all expenses, such as bills, subscriptions, and discretionary spending.

Step 2: Categorize Your Spending

Organize your expenses into:

- **Essential for survival** (e.g., rent, utilities, groceries).

- **Important but not essential** (e.g., transportation, gym membership, new laptop).
- **Wanted but not necessary** (e.g., dining out, entertainment, shopping).

Step 3: Review & Reflect

- Do you have money left after essential expenses?
- Are you saving, or are you over budget?
- What would your expenses look like if you only included essentials?
- Are there expenses that don't add meaningful value to your life?

Step 4: Experiment & Adjust

- Cut a non-essential expense for one week.
- Reflect: Did this impact your life significantly? Was it manageable?
- Try small changes, like opting for store-brand items instead of name-brand.

Step 5: Commit to Financial Awareness

- Regularly review your spending habits.
- Adjust your expenses to align with your needs and values.
- Use this exercise as a tool to build a financially sustainable and meaningful lifestyle.

By tracking and adjusting your spending, you take control of your finances, ensuring that your money supports what truly matters.

7.3 AVOIDING BURNOUT: STOIC PRACTICES FOR SUSTAINABLE LIVING

In today's fast-paced world, burnout has become a common plight for many. Overcommitment and a lack of balance between work and personal life are major contributors. You might find yourself juggling numerous responsibilities, each demanding your time and energy until the scales tip and exhaustion sets in. Emotional burnout manifests as a depletion of your mental resources, leading to decreased performance and a sense of detachment. You may feel like you're running on empty, your passion for work and life dimmed by the demands placed upon you. Recognizing these symptoms early on is key to addressing burnout before it takes a toll on your health and happiness.

To prevent burnout, Stoicism offers a toolkit of strategies focused on maintaining well-being. Setting boundaries is crucial. Learn to say no to commitments that don't align with your priorities. This doesn't mean shirking responsibilities but recognizing your limits and making mindful choices about where to direct your energy. If you want to revisit the importance of this, see Chapter 6 (6.8).

A common misunderstanding in life is the belief that we must constantly please others, often at the expense of our own well-being. However, this effort is futile—we cannot control what others think, feel, or do. While we can offer support through empathy and active listening, we cannot force change or influence their emotions. The key is to let people be as they are and stop exhausting ourselves, trying to meet everyone's expectations. Instead, prioritize self-care as a non-negotiable part of your life.

Some may see this approach as selfish, but it is not. Caring for your own well-being ensures that you can show up as your best self for friends, family, and daily challenges. When you take care of yourself, you meet life with poise and composure, staying aligned with your values rather than reacting out of exhaustion or frustration.

Self-care is often misrepresented as bubble baths and spa music—though those may be helpful ways for some to unwind. Proper self-care, however, is about recognizing and honoring your needs in different situations, relationships, and contexts. It means asking yourself, *What do I need to protect my well-being?* Sometimes, this might involve declining a social event because you recognize that rest is more important. While this may disappoint others temporarily, their emotions are not within your control, and disappointment is something people are fully capable of handling.

By staying in tune with your wants and needs, you build resilience, self-awareness, and the ability to act in alignment with your values. Self-care is not about avoidance or indulgence; it is about setting boundaries and making choices that sustain you in the long term.

A prevalent misconception in today's 24/7 work culture is that longer hours equate to greater success, with many believing they need to feel exhausted by the end of the working week. This belief is not only misleading but also poses significant health risks. The World Health Organization (WHO) reported that in 2016, over 745,000 deaths from stroke and ischemic heart disease were linked to working 55 hours or more per week, which is a 29% increase since 2000. Recent studies continue to highlight the dangers of excessive work hours. A 2021 systematic analysis found that long working hours are associated with an increased risk of cardiovascular diseases, including coronary heart disease and stroke. Recent studies continue to highlight the dangers of excessive work hours.

The human brain isn't designed for continuous work; disengagement from tasks is vital for both productivity and health. Contrary to the notion that breaks are unproductive, regular pauses during the workday and taking annual vacations are essential. Studies have shown that prolonged working hours can lead to increased stress levels, poor eating habits, lack of physical activity, and, ultimately, illness.

To promote long-term well-being, it is crucial to establish sustainable habits that incorporate regular breaks. Scheduling short pauses throughout your day allows for moments to breathe, reflect, and regain composure. Engaging in leisure activities, such as walking in nature, reading, or pursuing hobbies, provides a necessary balance to work demands. Embracing moderation and avoiding extremes ensures you have the energy to maintain your commitments over time. Mindful engagement in tasks fosters a deeper connection to your work, making even routine activities more meaningful and fulfilling.

As you navigate the challenges of modern life, remember that burnout is not an inevitable consequence of ambition. By adopting Stoic practices, you can maintain balance and fulfillment in your personal and professional endeavors. The journey to sustainable living begins with mindful choices and intentional actions. Embrace these practices, and you'll discover a path that not only prevents burnout but enriches your life with purpose and joy.

Practical Activity: Balancing Work and Rest

Purpose: Evaluate your work-rest balance, identify areas for improvement, and implement small changes to recharge effectively.

Step 1: Track Your Routine (One Week)

Monitor your daily activities, focusing on:

- When did you take a true break?
- What kind of break was it? (e.g., walking, meditation, exercise, TV)
- Did it help you feel replenished?
- Did you engage in activities outside of work that you genuinely enjoy?

Step 2: Reflect on Your Observations

- Did you allow enough time for real rest and recovery?
- Were your chosen breaks effective in boosting energy?
- How balanced do you feel at the end of the week?

Step 3: Adjust for the Upcoming Week

Make small but meaningful changes:

- **Nature Breaks:** Spend at least 15 minutes outdoors daily.
- **Enjoyable Activities:** Schedule time for hobbies or things you love.
- **Set Boundaries:** Define work-free periods, especially if working from home.

At the end of the following week, reflect on the following:

- Did these changes improve your energy levels?
- Do you feel more balanced and refreshed?

By consistently making small adjustments, you'll create a sustainable balance between work and rest, leading to better well-being.

7.4 THE ROLE OF TECHNOLOGY: DIGITAL TOOLS FOR STOIC PRACTICE

In the ever-evolving digital age, technology offers unprecedented opportunities to engage with ancient philosophies like Stoicism. The accessibility and convenience of digital tools can significantly enhance your Stoic practice, bringing a wealth of resources right to your fingertips. Imagine having access to the profound teachings of Marcus Aurelius or Seneca at any moment, delving into their wisdom during a quiet moment on the subway or while sipping your morning coffee. Online platforms provide access to a vast library of

Stoic literature, allowing you to explore texts and commentaries that deepen your understanding and appreciation of the philosophy. Although this journey has focused more specifically on practices to develop in response to 21st-century problems, there is much more to be learned about Stoicism. You may have found a section of this book that has particularly resonated with you or a specific Stoic teacher you want to learn more about. These resources are not limited to books alone; they include podcasts, articles, and discussions that can enrich your Stoic journey.

Moreover, technology facilitates virtual connections with fellow Stoics around the globe, transcending geographical limitations and fostering a sense of community. Through forums, discussion groups, and social media platforms, you can engage in thoughtful conversations, exchange insights, and gain fresh perspectives on Stoic teachings. This interconnectedness allows for collaboration and shared learning, where the diversity of ideas enriches your practice, just as ancient Stoics conversed in the bustling marketplaces of Athens or the grand forums of Rome.

For those looking to integrate digital tools into their Stoic practice, there are a variety of apps and platforms designed to support different elements of your journey. Meditation and mindfulness apps regularly incorporate Stoic principles, offering guided sessions that focus on cultivating presence and reducing unproductive thoughts. These apps provide a space for daily reflection, helping you center your mind and align your actions with Stoic virtues. Additionally, online courses and webinars on Stoic philosophy are available through a range of platforms, offering structured learning experiences that delve into the teachings of Stoic philosophers. These courses provide a comprehensive understanding of Stoicism, complete with interactive elements and opportunities for reflection, allowing you to engage deeply with the material.

Incorporating these digital tools into your daily life can be both practical and transformative. Consider setting reminders on your phone for daily reflections or meditation sessions, ensuring that Stoic practices become a consistent part of your routine. Digital journals also offer a convenient way to track your thoughts and goals, allowing you to evaluate your actions against Stoic virtues like wisdom, courage, and self-discipline. These journals can serve as a personal record of your growth, providing insights into your progress and areas for improvement. You are also able to store your values so that they are easily accessible at any moment. As you engage with these tools, they enhance your understanding of Stoicism and provide a sense of continuity and purpose in your practice.

However, it remains essential that you balance technology with mindful engagement. In a world full of digital distractions, staying focused on Stoic mindfulness takes intention and discipline. Set boundaries on screen time so technology serves your growth, not your distraction. Prioritize quality over quantity in digital interactions, engaging only with content that aligns with your values.

With a Stoic mindset, technology becomes a tool for growth while keeping you present. The digital world offers vast opportunities, but the goal remains personal growth and resilience. By blending ancient wisdom with modern tools, you navigate the complexities of today with clarity and purpose, fostering a fulfilling life beyond the screen.

Practical Activity: Exploring Digital Tools for Stoic Practices

Take some time to explore digital tools that can help you store and reflect on your values. Start by considering simple options like the Notes app on your phone, where you can quickly reflect and revisit them anytime.

Next, explore mindfulness and reflection apps such as Calm or Headspace, which can help you integrate regular reflection and mindfulness into your daily routine. These apps often include guided meditations and reflections that can support your mental clarity and emotional well-being.

Additionally, look into journaling apps that allow you to store your reflections digitally. These apps provide a convenient way to capture your thoughts and insights in a structured way, enabling you to complete this whenever it fits into your schedule.

Consider any other digital tools that can enhance your practice of self-reflection and mindfulness, making it easier to stay connected with your values and continue your personal growth journey.

7.5 THE SIGNIFICANCE OF COMMUNITY

The importance of community in Stoicism cannot be overstated. While the philosophy emphasizes introspection and self-reliance, it also values shared learning and collective wisdom. Engaging with others on the Stoic path provides space for dialogue, reflection, and accountability. Within this space, you find encouragement to push beyond your limits, knowing others walk alongside you. A strong community fosters resilience, offering support and empathy to navigate life's challenges. It serves as a mirror, reflecting the shared human experience and reminding you that you are not alone in your struggles or triumphs.

Building a Stoic support network requires actively seeking connections with like-minded individuals. Joining local Stoic meetups offers opportunities for thoughtful discussions, shared insights, and deeper exploration of Stoic concepts. Different perspectives enrich understanding, strengthening your practice. For those without access to in-person groups, online forums provide a valuable alternative. Platforms like Reddit and Facebook host vibrant communities where individuals exchange ideas, offer support, and discuss Stoicism's practical applications. These digital spaces ensure that Stoic wisdom remains accessible to all, fostering a global community of shared learning.

For those inspired to take a more active role, organizing and leading Stoic discussion groups can be deeply rewarding. Building such a community starts with clear goals and expectations. Begin with a small group, focusing on specific topics or texts that resonate with members. Structuring meetings with set agendas ensures purposeful discussions, allowing participants to explore the nuances of Stoic teachings. Encouraging open dialogue and diverse perspectives fosters an inclusive environment where all voices are heard and valued, enriching conversations and strengthening community bonds. Leading a group requires commitment, but the benefits are immense—you'll deepen your understanding of Stoicism, develop leadership skills, and positively impact others.

The benefits of a Stoic community extend beyond discussion. Engaging with others strengthens your commitment to Stoic principles and offers fresh perspectives on their application in daily life. Sharing experiences fosters connection, reinforcing the idea that personal growth is a shared journey. A strong community also serves as a source of motivation and encouragement, helping you persevere in your practice. The collective wisdom within the group becomes a wellspring of support, guiding you through life's complexities with greater clarity, resilience, and grace.

Practical Activity: Starting Your Stoic Discussion Group

If you're interested in starting a Stoic discussion group, here are some steps to help you get started:

1. **Find a Space**: Reach out to local libraries, community centers, or cafes to inquire about reserving a space for meetings.
2. **Gauge Interest**: Use social media or community boards to gauge interest and invite potential members.
3. **Choose a Topic**: For your first meeting, select a book or theme, such as Marcus Aurelius's *Meditations* or the Stoic principle of the dichotomy of control.
4. **Prepare an Agenda**: Create an agenda that includes discussion questions, personal reflection time, and space for

open sharing. This will ensure a balanced and engaging conversation.

5. **Foster Respect and Openness**: Encourage members to share their thoughts and experiences in a supportive, respectful environment.
6. **Expand and Evolve**: As the group grows, consider adding new formats, such as guest speakers or workshops, to keep the discussions dynamic and engaging.

By connecting with others who share your commitment to Stoicism, your group will become a space for meaningful reflection, deep learning, and the practical application of Stoic wisdom in daily life.

In concluding our exploration of overcoming modern life's challenges, consider how these Stoic principles and practices can be woven into the fabric of your daily existence. In the final chapter, we will explore how Stoic philosophers evolved over time and their key teachings that will serve as a foundation for the journey ahead. Before moving on, reflect on the final quote of the chapter below.

> *"We are all born for cooperation, as are the feet, the hands, the eyelids, and the upper and lower rows of teeth. To act against one another, then, is contrary to nature."*
>
> — MUSONIUS RUFUS, LECTURES, 9

8
PROFILES OF STOIC PHILOSOPHERS

"It is not that we have a short time to live, but that we waste a lot of it."

— SENECA, ON THE SHORTNESS OF LIFE

Critical to the development of Stoicism are the figures who embraced, taught, and shaped the approaches throughout many years. In this chapter, we will explore some of the most profound figures in Stoicism. This chapter is meant to give context to some of the practices that you have been exploring thus far and offer an introduction or signpost for further study into a philosopher of interest.

8.1 MARCUS AURELIUS: THE PHILOSOPHER KING

Imagine standing in a vast marble hall, its grandeur reflecting the weight of history. At the helm of this empire, amidst the whispers of power and responsibility, stands Marcus Aurelius, a man whose life was a tapestry woven with threads of philosophy and leadership. Born into a world of privilege in 121 AD, Marcus was groomed for greatness from an early age. He ascended to the position of Roman Emperor in 161 AD, a role that would test his commitment to Stoic principles amid the complexities of ruling one of history's greatest empires. His reign coincided with a period of significant challenge, marked by wars, plagues, and political intrigue. Yet, through it all, Marcus remained steadfast, guided by a commitment to Stoic ideals that emphasized duty, virtue, and rationality.

The personal reflections captured in his work, *Meditations*, offer a window into the mind of a ruler striving to live by Stoic virtues. These notes, written between 170 and 180 AD, were not intended for publication but as a means for self-improvement and philosophical exploration. In *Meditations*, Marcus Aurelius grapples with themes of duty, wrestling with the weight of his responsibilities while maintaining a focus on personal virtue. He reflects on the transient nature of power and life, urging himself to act justly and wisely in the face of adversity. His writings reveal a man who, despite the burdens of leadership, sought to understand and embrace the world through the lens of reason and humility.

Marcus Aurelius's contributions to Stoic philosophy are profound, particularly in how he integrated Stoic ethics into leadership. His reign exemplified the application of Stoic principles to governance, emphasizing inner strength and resilience. He viewed leadership as a service, a duty to uphold justice and virtue rather than to seek personal gain. His approach to governance was deeply rooted in Stoic thought, advocating for the welfare of his people and the integrity of the empire. Marcus's emphasis on self-discipline and rationality set a standard for future leaders, demonstrating the power of philosophy in shaping effective and ethical leadership.

The legacy of Marcus Aurelius extends far beyond his time, influencing countless thinkers and leaders throughout history. Contemporary leaders continue to draw inspiration from his Stoic approach, finding guidance in his reflections on resilience and virtue. His impact on Western philosophy is profound, with *Meditations* serving as a timeless guide for those seeking to navigate the complexities of life with wisdom and grace. The principles he embraced resonate with modern readers, offering insights into the pursuit of a life well-lived, grounded in the pursuit of virtue and understanding.

Key quote to reflect upon:

> *"Whoever values peace of mind and the health of the soul will live the best of all possible lives."*
>
> — MARCUS AURELIUS, MEDITATIONS

8.2 SENECA: THE STOIC STATESMAN

Imagine the bustling heart of Ancient Rome, a city teeming with ambition and intrigue, where the corridors of power were as perilous as they were promising. It was in this dynamic and often treacherous world that Seneca the Younger was born. Raised in a family that valued learning, Seneca's early life was steeped in education. He was introduced to Stoicism by his father, Seneca the Elder, and soon developed a profound appreciation for its teachings. This philosophical foundation would guide him throughout a career marked by both influence and controversy. As a statesman, Seneca served as an advisor to Emperor Nero, a role that placed him at the center of Roman politics. His tenure was fraught with challenges as he navigated the complexities of court life and the unpredictable moods of the emperor. Despite the turbulence, Seneca remained committed to Stoic principles, striving to balance his philosophical ideals with the demands of political life.

Seneca's writings offer a profound exploration of Stoic thought, providing practical insights into ethical living. Among his most notable works, *Letters to Lucilius* and *On the Shortness of Life* stand out for their timeless wisdom. *Letters to Lucilius* serves as a philosophical diary, covering topics from ethics to time's fleeting nature. Seneca urges readers to value each moment, manage time wisely, and avoid distractions that lead to an unfulfilled life. *On the Shortness of Life* expands on this theme, emphasizing the brevity of existence and the need to focus on what truly matters. Through these works, Seneca presents a vision of ethical living rooted in self-awareness and intentionality.

In his practical Stoicism, Seneca offers strategies for dealing with the challenges of wealth and power. Though he was a man of considerable means, Seneca understood that true contentment comes not from external possessions but from inner tranquility. He advised against the pursuit of material wealth for its own sake, warning of the emptiness that often accompanies such endeavors. Instead, Seneca encouraged a focus on cultivating virtues and finding fulfillment in simplicity and moderation. When faced with adversity, he advocated for a mindset of resilience, viewing misfortune as an opportunity for growth. He believed that by accepting life's trials with equanimity, one could transform challenges into stepping stones toward wisdom.

Seneca's impact on Stoicism and subsequent philosophical thought is profound, though not without its critics. His influence extends to later philosophers and writers who found inspiration in his teachings on virtue and resilience. However, Seneca's life was not without controversy. His substantial wealth and political actions have been scrutinized, leading some to question the consistency of his Stoic ideals with his personal choices. Critics point to his accumulation of wealth as contradictory to his philosophical teachings on simplicity and detachment. Despite these critiques, Seneca's writings continue to resonate with readers, offering a timeless exploration of the human condition and the pursuit of a meaningful life.

The legacy of Seneca is a testament to the enduring power of Stoic philosophy. His works invite us to reflect on the nature of time, the pursuit of virtue, and the capacity for resilience in the face of life's inevitable challenges. As you ponder Seneca's teachings, consider how his insights might inform your understanding of ethical living and the cultivation of inner peace. His reflections on time and mortality remind us to cherish each moment, embracing the present with gratitude and purpose.

Key quote to reflect upon:

"We suffer more in imagination than in reality."

— SENECA, LETTERS TO LUCILIUS

8.3 EPICTETUS: THE FORMERLY ENSLAVED PERSON WHO TAUGHT EMPERORS

Imagine the bustling streets of Hierapolis in the Roman Empire, where traders and philosophers filled the air with their voices. Amid this vibrant scene, Epictetus was born into slavery around 55 AD. His early life was marked by hardship, serving in Rome under Epaphroditus, a wealthy freedman of Emperor Nero. Yet, even in bondage, he found strength in philosophy. His master allowed him to study under Musonius Rufus, a Stoic philosopher who profoundly shaped his thinking. Eventually, Epictetus gained his freedom and dedicated himself entirely to philosophy. His experiences in slavery deeply informed his teachings, giving him a unique understanding of suffering and resilience.

Epictetus's philosophy, recorded in *The Discourses* and *The Enchiridion*, centers on the dichotomy of control, a core Stoic principle. He taught that while we control our thoughts, intentions, and reactions, external events and others' actions lie beyond our influence. Understanding this distinction helps reduce anxiety and fosters inner peace. By urging individuals to align with nature and reason, he provided practical guidance for navigating life's challenges. He emphasized integrity, self-discipline, and living in accordance with one's true nature. For Epictetus, true freedom was not physical but mental—achieved through mastering these philosophical principles.

The impact of Epictetus's teachings extended far beyond his own life, profoundly influencing both his contemporaries and future generations. He established a school in Nicopolis, where he taught philosophy to students who would go on to become leaders and philosophers themselves. His emphasis on personal freedom and the correct use of impressions resonated with many, offering a pathway to inner strength and clarity. The ideas he championed spread through his devoted students, who continued to propagate his teachings across the Roman world. Even those in positions of power, including future emperors, sought guidance from his wisdom, recognizing the value of Stoic principles in governance and personal conduct.

Epictetus's legacy endures, and his teachings continue to influence modern self-help and therapy. Cognitive-behavioral therapy (CBT), a widely used psychological treatment, draws heavily on Stoic ideas, particularly the emphasis on controlling one's thoughts and responses to external events. His philosophy underscores the importance of perception in shaping our experiences, a concept that aligns closely with the principles of CBT. Numerous individuals have found inspiration in Epictetus's teachings, using them to transform their lives and overcome personal challenges. This approach empowers individuals to navigate life's complexities with resilience and clarity, demonstrating the timeless relevance of Stoic wisdom.

Epictetus's journey from slavery to philosophical prominence illustrates a profound truth: that true freedom lies not in external circumstances but within our own minds. His teachings continue to offer guidance for those seeking to live with purpose and integrity, reminding us that while life may present challenges, our responses remain within our control.

Key quote to reflect upon:

"It's not what happens to you, but how you react to it that matters."

— EPICTETUS, DISCOURSES

8.4 MUSONIUS RUFUS: THE TEACHER OF PRACTICAL STOICISM

In the bustling streets of Ancient Rome, where the echoes of philosophy mingled with the everyday clamor of city life, Musonius Rufus stood as a beacon of Stoic wisdom. Known as one of the most practical Stoic philosophers, Musonius dedicated his life to teaching and advocating for a form of Stoicism that was deeply grounded in daily realities. Born in the 1st century CE, Musonius's upbringing was steeped in the rich traditions of Stoic thought. His education under renowned teachers equipped him with a profound understanding of Stoic principles, which he later imparted to his students. Musonius's role in Ancient Rome was not just as a philosopher but as an educator who believed in the transformative power of philosophy to improve the human condition. His teachings focused on the importance of living a life of virtue, grounded in ethical conduct and self-discipline. He viewed Stoicism not as an abstract theory but as a practical guide to navigating the challenges of everyday life.

Musonius Rufus's teachings were characterized by their practical application, emphasizing simplicity and ethical living. He advocated for a lifestyle that prioritized virtue over material wealth, urging his followers to focus on what truly mattered. Musonius believed that living a simple life was a path to true happiness and contentment, as it allowed individuals to align their actions with their values. His lessons on personal conduct highlighted the importance of self-discipline, encouraging individuals to exercise control over their desires and impulses. For Musonius, self-discipline was not about denying oneself pleasure but about making choices that fostered growth and integrity. He taught that by practicing moderation and restraint, one could cultivate a life rich in virtue and fulfillment.

Musonius Rufus also held progressive views on social issues, particularly concerning gender equality and education. At a time when women were often excluded from formal education, Musonius championed the idea that women should be educated alongside men. He argued that both men and women possessed the same capacity for reason and virtue and, therefore, deserved equal opportunities for learning. This belief in the equal education of women was revolutionary, challenging the prevailing norms of his time. Musonius emphasized that virtue was not just a private matter but one that extended to public life, advocating for ethical conduct in all spheres. His teachings encouraged individuals to engage with society in a way that was just and fair, promoting the idea that personal virtue contributed to the greater good.

The legacy of Musonius Rufus is evident in the impact he had on his students and subsequent Stoic thinkers. His influence on Epictetus, one of his most famous students, is particularly notable. Epictetus's teachings reflect the emphasis on practical Stoicism and ethical living that he learned from Musonius. Through his students, Musonius's ideas continued to spread, shaping the development of Stoic philosophy in the years that followed. In modern times, there is a renewed appreciation for Musonius's practical and ethical teachings. His insights into living simply and ethically resonate with contemporary audiences seeking a more mindful and intentional way of life. Musonius's advocacy for gender equality also aligns with modern values, highlighting the timeless relevance of his philosophy. His approach to Stoicism offers a blueprint for living a life of integrity and purpose, reminding us that the pursuit of virtue is a worthwhile and rewarding endeavor.

Key quote to reflect upon:

> *"The wise man does not let himself be ruled by his desires; he keeps them in check and remains in control of his actions."*
>
> — MUSONIUS RUFUS, LECTURES

8.5 HIEROCLES: THE STOIC'S GUIDE TO COMMUNITY AND CONNECTION

In the vibrant milieu of ancient Stoicism, Hierocles emerges as a significant figure whose teachings continue to resonate in discussions of community and ethics. As a prominent Stoic philosopher, Hierocles's life was devoted to exploring the dynamics of human connection and societal well-being. His background within the Stoic school positioned him as an influential voice, crafting philosophical insights that bridged personal ethics with communal responsibilities. His writings emphasize the interdependence between individuals and the communities they inhabit, arguing for a life lived in harmony with others. Hierocles's focus on ethics and interconnectedness offers a nuanced understanding of how personal virtues can extend beyond the self, creating a ripple effect that enhances the collective good.

Central to Hierocles's philosophy is the idea of the circles of concern, a metaphor illustrating how individuals can expand their empathy and connection to encompass broader communities. This concept begins with the self at the center, surrounded by concentric circles representing family, friends, fellow citizens, and ultimately, all humanity. The Stoic principle of oikiosis—affinity and belonging—underpins this model, encouraging individuals to cultivate connections that transcend immediate relationships. By consciously widening these circles, one can foster a more inclusive and compassionate worldview. Hierocles believed that by recognizing our shared humanity, we strengthen the bonds of society and promote a spirit of cooperation and mutual respect.

Hierocles's lessons on community and relationships are profound, highlighting the pivotal role of personal ethics in societal well-being. He advocated for a life guided by virtues such as wisdom, justice, and kindness, emphasizing their transformative power in fostering harmonious interactions. Hierocles taught that ethical living is not confined to personal conduct but extends into our communal engagements. Strategies for fostering connection and cooperation include active listening, open communication, and a willingness to understand diverse perspectives. By embracing these practices, individuals contribute to a culture of empathy and collaboration that benefits the entire community.

The influence of Hierocles on Stoic thought and beyond is significant. His ideas on community have permeated philosophical developments, inspiring subsequent thinkers to explore the ethical dimensions of human connection. Hierocles's emphasis on interdependence and shared responsibility continues to resonate in contemporary discussions of community building and social justice. In today's interconnected world, his teachings offer valuable insights into fostering inclusive and supportive communities. By embracing the principles of oikiosis and the circles of concern, individuals can cultivate a sense of belonging that transcends cultural and societal barriers, promoting a more compassionate and united world.

Hierocles's contributions to Stoicism serve as a reminder of the importance of community in personal and societal flourishing. His teachings underscore the value of extending our concern beyond the self, fostering connections that enrich both individual lives and the collective whole. As you reflect on Hierocles's ideas, consider how you might apply these principles to your own life. How can you expand your circles of concern to include those around you? What steps can you take to cultivate empathy and cooperation within your community? By engaging with these questions, you create a foundation for meaningful relationships that reflect the enduring wisdom of Stoic philosophy.

Key quote to reflect upon:

> *"We must make the bonds of affection between ourselves and all humanity as strong as those that bind us to our immediate family."*
>
> — HIEROCLES

As we conclude this chapter on the lives and teachings of notable Stoic philosophers, consider how their insights can guide you in your own pursuit of a virtuous and meaningful life. Through their diverse contributions, these thinkers have illuminated the path to resilience, ethical living, and community connection.

CONCLUSION

As we come to the end of our journey through the transformative world of Stoicism, I want to reflect on the profound insights and practical wisdom we've explored together. Throughout this book, we've delved into the historical context of Stoicism, engaging in an introduction to the timeless teachings of ancient philosophers like Marcus Aurelius, Seneca, and Epictetus. We've examined the core principles that form the foundation of Stoic thought, from the dichotomy of control to the pursuit of virtue and the cultivation of emotional resilience.

However, this book is more than just a collection of philosophical concepts. It's a practical guide filled with exercises and real-life applications to help integrate Stoicism into daily life. These practices, rooted in centuries-old wisdom, remain profoundly relevant today. From mindful morning routines to techniques for handling criticism, regulating emotions, and setting boundaries, we've examined strategies to navigate the complexities of modern existence. By embracing these, you have the power to transform relationships, sharpen decision-making, and cultivate a greater sense of purpose and fulfillment.

As you reflect on the key takeaways from each chapter, I encourage you to remember that Stoicism is not a one-time fix but a lifelong journey of personal growth and wisdom. The dichotomy of control teaches us to focus on what we can influence while accepting what lies beyond our reach. The role of virtues guides us to make decisions aligned with our highest values, while the power of self-reflection and continuous learning enables us to adapt and thrive in an ever-changing world.

However, the benefits of Stoic practice extend far beyond the pages of this book. By cultivating emotional resilience, you equip yourself to face life's challenges with courage and grace. By improving your decision-making skills, you chart a course toward success and fulfillment, and by nurturing strong, authentic relationships, you create a network of support and inspiration that will carry you through even the most challenging times.

So, as you close this book, I invite you to see it not as an ending but as a beginning—a call to action to continue your Stoic practice and share your insights with others. Engage with the vibrant Stoic community, both in-person and online, and leverage the power of digital tools to deepen your understanding. Revisit this book in times of need, reflecting on the practices and refining them to your context. Most importantly, strive to embody Stoic values in your daily interactions, leading by example and inspiring positive change in those around you.

Writing this book has been a profound personal journey for me, one that has reaffirmed my passion for helping others navigate the complexities of modern life through the wisdom of Stoicism. I am grateful for your commitment to this transformative philosophy, and I am honored to have been a part of your journey. As you continue on this path of growth and self-discovery, remember the words of Marcus Aurelius: *"You have power over your mind - not outside events. Realize this, and you will find strength."*

May this book serve as a constant companion and guide, reminding you of your inner strength and the boundless potential that lies within you. Embrace the wisdom of Stoicism, and let it light your way toward a life of purpose, resilience, and joy. The journey ahead may be challenging at times, but with the tools and insights you've gained, I have no doubt that you will rise to meet every obstacle with courage, wisdom, and grace.

Thank you for joining me on this incredible adventure. May your Stoic practice continue to flourish, and may you find endless inspiration in the timeless wisdom of these ancient philosophers. Remember, the power to transform your life lies within you. Seize it, and never let go.

"As long as you live, keep learning how to live."

— SENECA, LETTERS TO LUCILIUS

MAKE A DIFFERENCE WITH YOUR REVIEW

Unlock the Power of Generosity

"A person's worth is measured by the good they do, not by what they have."
Marcus Aurelius

When we give without expecting anything in return, we not only help others, but we enrich our own lives. Would you help someone just like you—curious about Stoicism but unsure where to begin? My mission is to make Stoicism simple, practical, and accessible to all.

But to reach more people, I need your help.

Most people choose books based on reviews. Your words could be the reason someone discovers the power of Stoicism and applies it to their life. It costs nothing, takes less than a minute, and could change someone's journey. Your review could help...

- ...one more person find peace in chaos.
- ...one more reader gain the courage to face challenges.
- ...one more mind unlock the wisdom of ancient philosophy.
- ...one more life be transformed by the wisdom of Stoic principles.

To make a difference, simply scan the QR code below and leave a review:
If you love helping others, you're my kind of person. Thank you from the bottom of my heart!, Charlie Steele

https://www.amazon.com/dp/1068797738

REFERENCES

American Institute for Cancer Research. (2023, February 14). *What is habit stacking and why is it important?* https://www.aicr.org/resources/blog/what-is-habit-stacking-and-why-is-it-important/

Art of Manliness. (n.d.). *Reflections on Marcus Aurelius' "Meditations"*. https://www.artofmanliness.com/character/manly-lessons/meditations-first-reading-aurelius-meditations/

Ballislife. (n.d.). *Kobe Bryant "Muse" motivational workout mix & his 666 workout routine.* https://ballislife.com/kobe-bryant-muse-motivational-workout-mix-his-666-workout-routine/

Bradley Hook. (n.d.). *Bradley Hook: Resilience, mindfulness & performance.* https://bradleyhook.com

Business Insider. (2025, February 16). *Jack Dorsey's daily routine: Meditation, a 'wake me up' lemon drink, and 7-minute workouts.* https://www.businessinsider.com/jack-dorsey-daily-routine-block-twitter

Calm. (n.d.). *Calm.* Retrieved March 7, 2025, from https://www.calm.com

Centers for Disease Control and Prevention. (2021). *Worker fatigue.* Occupational Safety and Health Administration. https://www.osha.gov/worker-fatigue

Cleveland Clinic. (2023, March 15). *What is habit stacking, and why is it important?* https://health.clevelandclinic.org/habit-stacking

Choi, E., Kim, Y., & Lee, H. (2022). The relationship between gratitude and psychological well-being: The mediating effect of self-esteem and perceived stress. *Healthcare, 10*(12), 2439. https://doi.org/10.3390/healthcare10122439

Cleveland Clinic. (2022, December 1). *Habit stacking: How to build new habits by piggybacking on existing ones.* https://health.clevelandclinic.org/habit-stacking

Cohen, S., Janicki-Deverts, D., & Miller, G. E. (2007). Psychological stress and disease. *JAMA, 298*(14), 1685–1687. https://www.researchgate.net/publication/5918645

Cregg, D. R., & Cheavens, J. S. (2018). Gratitude interventions: Effective self-help? A meta-analysis of the impact on symptoms of depression and anxiety. *Journal of Happiness Studies, 21,* 317–345. https://www.ncbi.nlm.nih.gov/pmc/articles/PMC6188704/

Daily Stoic. (n.d.). *"Memento Mori": The reminder we all desperately need.* https://dailystoic.com/memento-mori/

Daily Stoic. (n.d.). *Marcus Aurelius quotes: 50 most impactful passages from the Meditations.* https://dailystoic.com/marcus-aurelius-quotes/

Daily Stoic. (n.d.). *Stoicism can help put criticism in perspective.* https://dailystoic.com/criticism/

Daily Stoic. (n.d.). *Stoicism and compassion: A false dichotomy.* https://dailystoic.com/stoic-compassion/

Emmons, R. A., & Stern, R. (2013). Gratitude as a psychotherapeutic intervention. *Journal of Clinical Psychology, 69*(8), 846–855. https://doi.org/10.1002/jclp.22020

Estoicismo.ar. (n.d.). *Stoicism and ethical leadership: Building trust through virtue.* https://estoicismo.ar/english/leadership/stoicism-and-ethical-leadership-building-trust-through-virtue/

Forbes. (2024, July 9). *A psychologist explains love's 5:1 ratio: Key to making any relationship work. Forbes.* https://www.forbes.com/sites/traversmark/2024/07/09/a-psychologist-explains-loves-51-ratio-key-to-making-any-relationship-work/

Frontiers in Psychology. (2019, July 17). *Mindfulness and well-being: A systematic review of meta-analyses. Frontiers in Psychology, 10*, 1556. https://www.frontiersin.org/articles/10.3389/fpsyg.2019.01556/full

Frontiers in Psychology. (2019, July 23). *The role of habits in self-control.* https://www.frontiersin.org/articles/10.3389/fpsyg.2019.01556/full

Goodreads. (n.d.). *Fortify yourself with contentment, for this is an impregnable fortress.* https://www.goodreads.com/quotes/1280375-fortify-yourself-with-contentment-for-this-is-an-impregnable-fortress

Goodreads. (n.d.). *I like to get ten pages a day, which amounts to 3,650 pages a year. That's ten or twelve books.* https://www.goodreads.com/quotes/49619-i-like-to-get-ten-pages-a-day-which-amounts

Goodreads. (n.d.). *Marcus Aurelius Quotes.* https://www.goodreads.com/author/quotes/17212.Marcus_Aurelius

Gottman Institute. (2013, May 9). *The magic relationship ratio, according to science.* https://www.gottman.com/blog/the-magic-relationship-ratio-according-science/

Greater Good Science Center. (2018, June 6). *How gratitude changes you and your brain.* University of California, Berkeley. https://greatergood.berkeley.edu/article/item/how_gratitude_changes_you_and_your_brain

Harvard University. (n.d.). *The science of social connection.* https://archive.blogs.harvard.edu/socialconnection/

Hauschild, J.-M., & Schulze, R. (2022). Decision-making and life satisfaction: The role of general decision-making styles and maximizing tendency as predictors. *Current Psychology*. Advance online publication. https://www.researchgate.net/publication/365731284

Headspace. (n.d.). *Headspace.* Retrieved March 7, 2025, from https://www.headspace.com

HelpGuide. (n.d.). *Benefits of mindfulness.* https://www.helpguide.org/mental-health/stress/benefits-of-mindfulness

Hirshberg, D. (2021, November 22). *This man found 1,650 ways to turn a profit while decarbonizing. WIRED.* https://www.wired.com/story/this-man-found-1650-ways-to-turn-a-profit-while-decarbonizing/

House, J. S., Landis, K. R., & Umberson, D. (1988). Social relationships and health. *Science, 241*(4865), 540–545. https://www.ncbi.nlm.nih.gov/pmc/articles/PMC3505409/

Internet Encyclopedia of Philosophy. (n.d.). *Stoic ethics.* https://iep.utm.edu/stoiceth/

Jaffe, E., Oh, D. H., Goldstein, M., & Zehtabchi, S. (2022). Association between emergency physician self-reported burnout and mortality among patients in the emergency department. *Academic Emergency Medicine, 29*(12), 1322–1329. https://doi.org/10.1111/acem.13967

Journey Cloud. (n.d.). *The 7 best Stoic apps to cultivate daily Stoicism.* https://blog.journey.cloud/7-best-stoic-apps-to-cultivate-daily-stoicism/

Killgore, W. D. S., Cloonan, S. A., Taylor, E. C., & Dailey, N. S. (2020). Loneliness: A signature mental health concern in the era of COVID-19. *Psychiatry Research, 290,* 113117. https://www.ncbi.nlm.nih.gov/pmc/articles/PMC6673057/

LifeHack. (2017, March 28). *Wealthy, successful people who choose less over more: 10 real life stories of minimalists.* https://www.lifehack.org/584538/wealthy-successful-people-who-choose-less-over-more-10-real-life-stories-of-minimalists

Making Caring Common Project. (2021). *Loneliness in America: How the pandemic has deepened an epidemic of loneliness and what we can do about it.* Harvard Graduate School of Education. https://mcc.gse.harvard.edu/reports/loneliness-in-america

McEwen, B. S. (2009). Protective and damaging effects of stress mediators: Central role of the brain. *Dialogues in Clinical Neuroscience, 11*(3), 273–289. https://pubmed.ncbi.nlm.nih.gov/19350430/

McLean, C. P., Su, Y.-J., & Foa, E. B. (2019). Mechanisms of prolonged exposure therapy for PTSD: Evidence from neuroimaging. *Biological Psychiatry: Cognitive Neuroscience and Neuroimaging, 4*(6), 556–563. https://www.ncbi.nlm.nih.gov/pmc/articles/PMC6302524/

Medium. (n.d.). *Amor Fati: Stoicism and the love of fate.* https://medium.com/@orion_philosophy/amor-fati-stoicism-and-the-love-of-fate-orion-philosophy-8f9ed65aed4d

Medium. (n.d.). *Amor Fati: Stoicism and the love of fate.* https://medium.com/@orion_philosophy/amor-fati-stoicism-and-the-love-of-fate-orion-philosophy-8f9ed65aed4d

Medium. (n.d.). *Epictetus on dealing with your own anger.* https://medium.com/practical-rationality/dealing-with-ones-own-anger-epictetus-advice-2bf3865504fc

Medium. (n.d.). *Stoic leadership: Timeless wisdom for modern decision-making.* https://medium.com/secular-wisdom/stoic-leadership-timeless-wisdom-for-modern-decision-making-4c97f7cdfe7d

Medium. (n.d.). *The daily routine of Marcus Aurelius (Updated 2023).* https://medium.com/mind-cafe/i-followed-marcus-aurelius-daily-routine-and-the-results-were-incredible-6b98ef52b6c5

Medium. (n.d.). *The resilience of adversity: Lessons from Seneca.* https://medium.com/@stoicminds.channel/the-resilience-of-adversity-lessons-from-seneca-9e1e4dbefad1

Mental Health Center. (n.d.). *The science behind gratitude and happiness.* https://www.mentalhealthctr.com/the-science-behind-gratitude-and-happiness/

Mind & Practice. (n.d.). *Stoic virtues & personal values to be your best self.* https://mindandpractice.com/be-your-best-self-with-personal-values-stoic-virtue/

Mindful Stoic. (n.d.). *Quotes on stoicism: Wisdom from the Stoic philosophers.* https://mindfulstoic.net/quotes-on-stoicism/

Michael Moody Fitness. (n.d.). *My 10 favorite life-guiding quotes from Marcus Aurelius.*

https://www.michaelmoodyfitness.com/personaltrainersfitnessanddietblog/my-10-favorite-life-guiding-quotes-from-marcus-aurelius

Modern Stoicism. (n.d.). *How to bring Stoicism to your city.* https://modernstoicism.com/how-to-bring-stoicism-to-your-city/

Modern Stoicism. (n.d.). *Stoicism and desire regulation by Ryan Bush.* https://modernstoicism.com/stoicism-and-desire-regulation-by-ryan-bush/

Modern Stoicism. (n.d.). *The Stoic love of community by Matt Van Natta.* https://modernstoicism.com/the-stoic-love-of-community-by-matt-van-natta/

MVP Mindset. (2020, August 23). *Kobe Bryant - Mamba mentality | Motivational video* [Video]. YouTube. https://www.youtube.com/watch?v=ym-o65Dub8c

Nguyen, T. T. H., & Gan, C. (2022). Maximizing tendency and decision-making styles as predictors of well-being. *Journal of Happiness Studies, 23*, 2031–2053. https://doi.org/10.1007/s10902-021-00440-y

Ophir, E., Nass, C., & Wagner, A. D. (2009). Cognitive control in media multitaskers. *Proceedings of the National Academy of Sciences, 106*(37), 15583–15587. https://doi.org/10.1073/pnas.0903620106

Owaves. (n.d.). *A day in the life: Serena Williams.* https://owaves.com/day-plan/day-life-serena-williams/

PubMed Central. (n.d.). *U.S. National Library of Medicine.* https://pmc.ncbi.nlm.nih.gov

Rozanski, A., Blumenthal, J. A., & Kaplan, J. (1998). Impact of psychological factors on the pathogenesis of cardiovascular disease and implications for therapy. *The New England Journal of Medicine, 338*(4), 246–253. https://doi.org/10.1056/NEJM199801153380307

Psyche. (n.d.). *Musonius Rufus: Roman Stoic, and avant-garde feminist?* https://psyche.co/ideas/musonius-rufus-roman-stoic-and-avant-garde-feminist

Routledge. (n.d.). *An analysis of Marcus Aurelius's Meditations - 1st edition.* https://www.routledge.com/An-Analysis-of-Marcus-Aureliuss-Meditations/Orr/p/book/9781912128396

Ryu, J. H., Kim, H., & Cho, S. S. (2021). Effect of long working hours on depression and mental health in occupational workers: A systematic review and meta-analysis. *International Journal of Environmental Research and Public Health, 18*(21), 11488. https://www.ncbi.nlm.nih.gov/pmc/articles/PMC8642716/

Schwarz, N., & Clore, G. L. (2007). Affect as information. In J. Forgas (Ed.), *Feeling and thinking: The role of affect in social cognition* (2nd ed., pp. 159–179). Psychology Press. https://www.researchgate.net/publication/292445684

Slavich, G. M., & Irwin, M. R. (2014). From stress to inflammation and major depressive disorder: A social signal transduction theory of depression. *Psychological Bulletin, 140*(3), 774–815. https://doi.org/10.1037/a0035302

Stanford Encyclopedia of Philosophy. (n.d.). *Epictetus.* https://plato.stanford.edu/entries/epictetus/

Stoic Buddy. (n.d.). *Ataraxia vs. Apatheia - Meanings and differences.* https://www.stoic-buddy.com/blog/ataraxia-vs-apatheia-meanings-and-differences/

Taylor, L. (2024, November 29). *Sarina Wiegman and Emma Hayes: Contrasting figures united by common empathy. The Guardian.* https://www.theguardian.com/football/

2024/nov/29/sarina-wiegman-and-emma-hayes-contrasting-figures-united-by-common-empathy

The Stoic Handbook. (n.d.). *Stoic quotes on anxiety.* https://www.stoichandbook.co/stoic-quotes-on-anxiety/

The Stoic Handbook. (n.d.). *The ultimate Stoic daily routine.* https://www.stoichandbook.co/ultimate-stoic-daily-routine/

The Week. (2016). *Wit & wisdom. The Week* (1062), 21.

University of Maryland Global Campus. (2022, November 22). *The science of gratitude. UMGC Blog.* https://www.umgc.edu/blog/the-science-of-gratitude

Wong, J., Kini, P., McInnis, S., Gabana, N., & Brown, J. W. (2016). The effects of gratitude expression on neural activity. *Social Cognitive and Affective Neuroscience, 11*(10), 1550–1557. https://doi.org/10.1093/scan/nsw093

Wood, A. M., Froh, J. J., & Geraghty, A. W. A. (2010). Gratitude and well-being: A review and theoretical integration. *Clinical Psychology Review, 30*(7), 890–905. https://www.ncbi.nlm.nih.gov/pmc/articles/PMC4193464/

World Health Organization. (2021, May 17). *Long working hours increasing deaths from heart disease and stroke: WHO, ILO.* https://www.who.int/news/item/17-05-2021-long-working-hours-increasing-deaths-from-heart-disease-and-stroke-who-ilo

World History Encyclopedia. (n.d.). *Zeno of Citium.* https://www.worldhistory.org/Zeno_of_Citium/

Printed in Great Britain
by Amazon

63326099R00090